HOUSE of GAMES

HOUSE of GAMES

QUESTION SMASH

1 3 5 7 9 10 8 6 4 2

BBC Books, an imprint of Ebury Publishing
20 Vauxhall Bridge Road,
London SW1V 2SA

BBC Books is part of the Penguin Random House group of companies
whose addresses can be found at global.penguinrandomhouse.com

Text copyright © Remarkable Television Ltd

Alan Connor has asserted his right to be identified as the author of this Work in
accordance with the Copyright, Designs and Patents Act 1988

First Published by BBC Books in 2022

www.penguin.co.uk

A CIP catalogue record for this book is available from the British Library

ISBN 9781785946721

Commissioning Editor: Yvonne Jacob
Editor: Bethany Wright
Design: Clarkevanmeurs Ltd and E-type Design

Printed and bound in Great Britain by Clays Ltd, Elcograf S.p.A.

MIX
Paper from
responsible sources
FSC® C018179

Penguin Random House is committed to a sustainable future
for our business, our readers and our planet. This book is
made from Forest Stewardship Council® certified paper.

CONTENTS

Introduction 6

SET 1 11
SET 2 25
SET 3 43
SET 4 61
SET 5 77
SET 6 91
SET 7 103
SET 8 117
SET 9 133
SET 10 149
SET 11 167
SET 12 179
SET 13 193
SET 14 205
SET 15 223
SET 16 235
SET 17 247
SET 18 257
SET 19 273
SET 20 287
SET 21 299
SET 22 317
SET 23 333
SET 24 349
SET 25 365
SET 26 381

One Last Thing 396
Credits 397
Index of Games 398

INTRODUCTION

ALAN CONNOR, QUESTION TINKERER: My favourite place in the House of Games is the water cooler on the balcony overlooking the Billiards Room. We gather there to take a break, to watch Stephen Hendry trying desperately hard to lose to Richard and, most of all, to switch off from writing quiz questions for ten minutes and enjoy a natter.

For example, I'll never forget the Monday morning after Emma Raducanu's US Open victory, when we were all devastated that the trophy had not gone to Emma's rival Leylah Fernandez. 'Fernandez' lends itself so much more readily to Rhyme Time.

And I have fond memories of the morning when someone got an alert to say that the new album from Adele would be named *30* and we sprinted back to our alcoves to be the first to use the information in one of our large sub-family of number-based games.

OK, let me be more honest with you. When I said 'to switch off from writing quiz questions', I could more accurately have put 'to pause from writing quiz questions in order to talk *about* quiz questions' – and to quiz each other.

And now we'd like to quiz you. If you're up for it.

There are some brand-new games, if you'd like to accompany us to the Martial Arts Room, which is where we do our game development. I'm not sure why we even have a Martial Arts Room; none of us are in the least martial, but the crash mats are lovely and comfy if you need a little lie down while you're trying to nail an exciting new pairs game.

We'll visit one of the Libraries, where we'll come up with some brand-new questions for as many as possible of the games you know from the TV show. We're not allowed to include the Mulled Wine Game as featured in the unbroadcast Christmas special, for reasons which will be incredibly obvious to anyone who's managed to find a copy of the recording on the dark web – but there are plenty of Answer Smashes, limericks and creative use of emojis.

And in the Conservatory, we'll recall some of our best-loved questions from the first six series and tell you some behind-the-scenes secrets and, if you're interested, our recommendations for the hottest, most authoritative reference books to be found on the open market. (I'm being told as I type that we will 'absolutely not' be sharing recommendations of reference books. Don't worry, readers: I'll make sure we give you those in book number three.)

Most of the games work well if you're in a little group and you can keep track of points using our little scorecards – or just dip in and out whenever you feel like quizzing. Sometimes you might need a pencil and paper, or a phone, but we'll explain all that at the start of each game.

So what shall we start with? Well, you know how Richard says, at the start of every Monday show, 'You don't know what game we're starting with, I don't know what game we're starting with'? This leaves me baffled, as nearly every Monday we start with Rhyme Time – you'd think he'd know how we put the shows together by now. We do this as we think it's a good way to begin things. So we've also done it in this book.

Have biscuits to hand and please quiz responsibly.

SET 1

... which is numbered '1'
but starts by talking about '2's

GAME 1
RHYME TIME

You need: no extra materials; just this book

Players: someone to read, and ideally 2 or more players

Scoring: 2 points for every correct answer

You know Rhyme Time. **You get a pair of clues. There's a pair of answers. And the answers rhyme.** Fred Astaire; Chocolate éclair. Chocolate spread; 'Can't Get You Out of My Head'. Chocolate soufflé; 'That'll Be the Day'. They don't have to involve chocolate, but the first few rhymes originated by any given member of the team tend to mention sweet and/or baked goods, on the principle of 'Write what you know'.

In fact, Rhyme Time doesn't usually use a theme at all, but since this is the start of the *House of Games* book number two, we'll mark that by using TWO as our theme.

If you're reading the clues, choose someone and read them the first pair; 2 points if they get both right; if not, pass it to the right until someone does, for 1 point.

Either way, play *then* passes to the right.

1. Biblical boat where animals entered 'two by two'

   Big open space in the middle of Manhattan

2. Name of *Strictly*'s spin-off show

   Name of a battle, a London station and Abba's Eurovision winner

3. White flower celebrated in *The Sound of Music*

   Sean Connery Bond film with a script by Roald Dahl

4. Teacher who might ask for a sun salutation or downward dog

   Two over par in golf

5. German tennis champ of the 1980s

   Bus you can walk upstairs in

6. Celine Dion's first UK number one

   More formal name for nits

7. Film with Elsa, Anna, Sven and Olaf but *not* 'Let It Go'

   Greeting offered by roosters

8.   'Family' of those roosters

Author of *A Tale of Two Cities*

9.   Cylindrical crisps that used to have a 'Big O's' variant

Usual name for the Victoria Wood sketch officially titled 'Waitress'

10. Netherlands-referencing term meaning 'nonsense'

Affliction whereby you turn everything to gold

ANSWERS
See page 22

GAME 2

A BLAST FROM THE PAST TENSE

You need: basic knowledge of the English language

Players: any number: take turns, passing the book around (no peeking ahead!)

Scoring: 2 points for every correct answer

Accompany us now, if you will, to the quietest room in the House of Games: the Rest Lounge for Retired Games.

Many viewers think fondly of this game. It's one of those ones where you don't give the actual answer: **you take any parts of the answer that could be put in the past tense, put them in the past tense and give that new mangled phrase as your answer.**

So, if we asked: 'Who starred as manipulative novelist Catherine Tramell in *Basic Instinct*?', you wouldn't get points for 'Sharon Stone', but you would for 'Sharon Stoned'.

However, you won't see A Blast From The Past Tense any more, because we feared we were running out of answers. Since everyone has a favourite round, and some of you will have obtained a copy of this book solely in order to play the past-tense game, we've assigned a crack team to find the very last few questions that fit the format. Enjoy! Savour them! And then say goodbye forever.

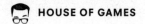

1. In the 1933 film, King Kong climbs up the *what* building?

2. Who played Regan in *The Sweeney*, Morse in *Inspector Morse* and Kavanagh in *Kavanagh QC*?

3. When people head off on a big journey to John O'Groats, where have they usually started?

4. Jason Donovan played drag artist Mitzi Mitosis in the original West End run of which musical?

5. Les Dennis, Chris Evans and Brian Blessed have provided the voices for which trio of cereal mascots?

6. Which Oscar-winning film-maker directed the 1992 film *Malcolm X*?

7. In *West Side Story*, what song is performed by Maria as she is getting ready for her tryst with Tony?

8. What was the three-word name of the uncouth canine puppet operated by Bob Carolgees?

9. What repetitive six-word phrase to introduce a joke was first recorded in the 1960s?

10. In the intro to Beats International's 'Dub Be Good to Me', what five words come before 'nitty-gritty'?

ANSWERS
See page 22

GAME 3
IMAGINARY CHARADES

You need: something to block off the
answers that haven't been asked yet

Players: any number

Scoring: 20 points to be divided up based on
whoever has made the bravest choices and moves

We are now in the Game History Room. As keen students, players and creators of games, we keep records of how various games came to be.

Charades, for example, was once an insufferably literary and often rhyming variant of those riddles that go 'My first is in "diddle"...'. I'd give you examples, but they would need so many footnotes to explain the obscure eighteenth-century references that we would have to offer this as a three-foot-high book.* Which would apparently be quite pricey.

The game evolved into the form we know best, where you mime the words or syllables of a TV show or song from musical theatre, etc., and reached its final form here in the House of Games when we realised how much more fun it is when **the TV shows and songs from musical theatre, etc., are completely made up.**

---

*   Go on then, here's a short one, by Jane Austen: 'My first is company; my second shuns company; my third collects company; and my whole amuses company.' It's an abbreviation for 'company' (CO), then someone who lives a secluded life (NUN), a way of drumming up interest (DRUM), so the whole thing is a puzzle (CONUNDRUM). Makes you glad she stuck to critiques of social sensibilities, right?

TITLES

(younger players: if you don't know some of the names
and words, just make up your own title instead)

1. Attacked by Porcupines (film)

2. The 3.55 from Basingstoke (whodunnit)

3. Surreptitious Glances and Condescending Winks (song)

4. Well, Someone Must Know Where My Mojo Is (theatrical farce)

5. The Bagel Under the Hatstand (film)

6. Britain's Slowest Chefs (TV competition)

7. 32 More Things to Do in the Northwest Passage (travel book)

8. Attacked by More Porcupines (film sequel)

9. St Francis of Assisi Stole My Lunch (celebrity memoir)

10. I Got Those Woke Up to Find Myself Transformed into a Gigantic Insect Blues (blues standard)

GAME 4
ANSWER SMASH

By the time the first readers of these words read them, we will have smashed a few thousand answers into a few thousand more.

Not for us, though, high-handedly to assume you know the format. **You'll be asked a question and shown an image, and you'll combine the answer with what's in the image to make a Smashed Answer.** So if the clue read 'Strictly dance that's like a faster, cheeky rumba' and there was an image of some charcoal, you would answer: Cha-cha-charcoal.

Remember, no points unless you successfully smash the answers together ...

Block off the page, gather round, reveal them one at a time and yell when you've got the answer.

1. What kind of shredded paper is traditionally thrown on to parades in New York City?

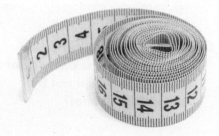

2. What kitchen implement is used to combine albumen and yolk?

3. What three-word phrase describes something light that broke a camel's back?

4. And what three-word describes Diego Maradona's controversial goal against England at the 1986 World Cup?

5. Movie star Steve McQueen was known by what flattering and regal nickname?

6. What abbreviation on an invitation warns party-goers that the host will not be providing alcohol?

7. Which 11-letter nonsense word can you use in place of a word that you've forgotten?

8. Which comic song of 1888 asks about the provenance of a piece of headgear?

9. In poetry, what precedes the words 'Whence all but he had fled'?

10. What order is given on a boat when it is time to take to the lifeboats?

ANSWERS

See page 22

ANSWERS

GAME 1: RHYME TIME

1. Noah's ark
   Central Park
2. *It Takes Two*
   Waterloo
3. Edelweiss
   You Only Live Twice
4. Yogi
   Double bogey
5. Boris Becker
   Double-decker
6. 'Think Twice'
   Head lice
7. *Frozen II*
   Cock-a-doodle-do
8. Chickens
   Charles Dickens
9. Hula Hoops
   Two Soups
10. Double Dutch
    Midas touch

GAME 2: A BLAST FROM THE PAST

1. Empire Stated
2. John Thawed
3. Landed's Ended (ask again if they say 'Land's Ended')
4. *Priscilla, Queen of the Deserted*
5. Snapped, Crackled and Popped
6. Spiked Lee

7. 'I Felt Pretty'
8. Spat the Dogged
9. I said, I said, I said
10. Tanked flew bossed walked jammed

GAME 4: ANSWER SMASH

1. Ticker tape measure
2. Egg whisky (or indeed egg whiskey!)
3. The last strawberry
4. Hand of Godysseus
5. The King of Coolbag
6. BYOBMX
7. Thingamajigsaw
8. 'Where Did You Get That Hatstand?'
9. 'The boy stood on the burning deckchair'
10. Abandon shipflask

SET 1 SCORECARD			
	Player 1	Player 2	Player 3	Player 4
Game 1				
Game 2				
Game 3				
Game 4				
Totals				

WINNER!

SET 2

... in which we curse our past selves

GAME 5

THE ANSWER'S IN THE QUESTION

You need: nothing

Players: any number

Scoring: 2 for each correct answer

For the first game in this set, we've been gentle and given you the answer *while giving you the clue.*

Just so there's some element of challenge, we've jumbled the answers. **The words in bold type can be rearranged to form the answer, which is also described by the clue as a whole.**

You'll probably want to gather round the book and do this together. But if you insist, someone can read them out and you can get competitive.

Incidentally, you might be wondering why we didn't use this name for Hidden In Plain Sight (Games 30 and 62), where the answer really is quite literally in the question.

It's because we thought of this game first and so when we came up with Hidden In Plain Sight, all we could do was sigh at the rash decisions made by our past selves. Curse you, past selves!

PART ONE

1. You can wear these for fashion or, if you're working in the **garden, use** them to protect your clothes underneath.

2. Mums everywhere declare: 'I have faith **in my son, daughter**, etc. not to forget me on this special day.'

3. This author's character Max decides to go on a **cruise and make** mischief with a band of Wild Things.

4. This hat aims to stop the rain from making its **user wet so** it has a lovely wide brim at the back.

5. Trapped with the suspects in this tale, Poirot sees them create **terror under his nose - exempt**, they hope, from being brought to justice.

Now maybe have a little break before Part Two?

PART TWO

1. The influence of this revolutionary has had more than a **vague reach** - his image is recognised across the world.

2. A forger, as part of a **con, emulated** this impressionist's renditions of haystacks and sold them around the world.

3. For his sporting prowess, this British decathlete was rewarded **handsomely, top** of the list being Olympic golds in 1980 and 1984.

4. Whether you run an English butcher's, a Welsh greengrocer's or an **Irish bakery**, these two bearded chaps would be welcome customers.

5. This writer's stories tend to **pose a** moral quandary and end with a tiresome little life lesson.

ANSWERS
See page 40

GAME 6

BUILD YOUR OWN QUESTION

You need: nothing

Players: 1 question-reader, 2 players or teams

Scoring: 1 point for every correct answer

You join us in the room where the *House of Games* team works on those games where a single question set might take over a day, but only a small fraction of the work ends up on the screen. Welcome to the Room of Gritted Teeth.

In Build Your Own Question, **the question-asker reads out the four categories along the columns, then the four down the rows.** (If the question-asker is you, you should insist that everyone writes down the categories, and ticks off what's been answered, unless you especially enjoy people later asking 'What are the categories again?' and 'Have we already had Types of Underwear and Booker Prize Winners?')

Taking it in turns, each player/team chooses one column category and one row category and the question-asker gives them the question that fits both. Unlike on the telly, repeat until all 16 questions have been asked and answered.

	Truth & Lies	Disaster Films
Coins	Which country is represented on a round pound coin with the words 'Pleidiol wyf i'm gwlad' ('True am I to my country')?	Fill the gap: Michael Caine tries to salvage treasure in an exciting movie sequel entitled *Beyond the _____ Adventure*.
Inventions	The lie detector was invented by a psychologist who also invented which tiara-sporting, lasso-wielding superhero?	Flint Lockwood invents a machine that transforms water to food in a film called *Cloudy with a Chance of ...* what?
Double Acts	'Truth is only that which is taken to be true' is a line from which double-act Tom Stoppard play?	In 1998, French and Saunders performed a memorable parody of which lucrative romantic maritime blockbuster?
Libraries	Books with labels in the 800s are generally fiction in which library cataloguing system?	Which 2004 climate disaster flick sees Jake Gyllenhaal stranded in the New York Public Library?

Rabbits	Ice Cream	
In 2016, Peter Rabbit appeared on which seven-sided coin?	When serving ice cream, the cone replaced what unsavoury piece of glass, passed from customer to customer?	**Coins**
Lapine is a language invented for the rabbits of which 1972 novel?	An invention at the 1904 World's Fair in St Louis served ice cream in which familiar geometric shape?	**Inventions**
In Morecambe and Wise's 1973 Christmas show, Ernie hid rabbits in his tunic for a diminutive portrayal of which French despot?	Cheese and onion ice cream features in a sketch by which 1970s comedy duo who shared a first name?	**Double Acts**
Whose roles have included Ethel in *On Golden Pond*, Rose in *The African Queen* and the librarian Bunny in *Desk Set*?	The US Library of Congress holds a recipe for ice cream created by which American president named Thomas?	**Libraries**

ANSWERS

	Truth & Lies	Disaster Films	Rabbits	Ice Cream
Coins	Wales	*Beyond the Poseidon Adventure*	The 50 pence	The penny lick
Inventions	Wonder Woman*	*Meatballs*	*Watership Down*	Ice cream cone
Double Acts	*Rosencrantz and Guildenstern are Dead*	*Titanic*	Napoleon	*The Two Ronnies*
Libraries	Dewey	*The Day After Tomorrow*	Katharine Hepburn	Jefferson

---

* William Moulton Marston's Harvard dissertation was titled 'Systolic blood pressure symptoms of deception and constituent mental states'.

GAME 7
BROKEN KARAOKE

If you're reading the questions, first give the year. Then **read out the initials to the lyrics from a well-known passage in a well-known pop song.** Try to match them to the song – for example, if the song contains a very long 'yeeeeeeeeeaaaaaaaaaaaaah', say a curt, simple 'Y', then wait until giving the next letter.

TRY TO STAY ON ONE NOTE. This is not a game about melody. It's pure words, all the way.

If you don't know a song, skip it (or just give it your best shot on the basis that it's not your problem).

And if they don't get it the first time, just read it again, and again …

1. *Year: 1963*   S L Y
                       Y Y Y
                       S L Y
                       Y Y Y
                       W A L L T
                       Y K Y S B G

2. *Year: 1996*   O A J A L B
                      O A A L B M
                      O A J A L B
                      Y K W I L F

3. *Year: 1993*   A I W D A F L
                      O I W D A F L
                      I W D A F L
                      B I W D T
                      N I W D T

4. *Year: 1995*   I S M (I S M)
                      Y G B T O T S M (T S M)
                      A A A
                      Y M W

5. *Year: 2018*   B S
                      D D D D D D D
                      B S
                      D D D D D D D
                      B S
                      D D D D D D D
                      B S

ANSWERS
See page 40

GAME 8
THE Z LIST

You need: pencil and paper for each player; a stopwatch if you think you need to be strict about time

Players: any number

Scoring: see below

Two more games that we tend to muddle up are Z-A (where the letters appear in reverse alphabetical order: not possible in book form for another year or so, claims the House of Games's department of Rhubarb and Delay [R&D]), and this game: The Z List.

Here, you get 1 point if your answer fits the category, 3 points if yours is the last alphabetically of everyone playing and 5 points if yours is the answer that comes last alphabetically of all the acceptable answers that we kindly provide. Cover up the possible answers.

Ignore, please, any 'The's or 'A's etc. at the beginning of possible answers. That's standard.

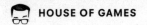

PIXAR FEATURE FILMS

Brave	Incredibles, The	Soul
Bug's Life, A	Incredibles 2	Toy Story
Cars	Inside Out	Toy Story 2
Cars 2	Lightyear	Toy Story 3
Cars 3	Luca	Toy Story 4
Coco	Monsters, Inc.	Turning Red
Finding Dory	Monsters University	Up
Finding Nemo	Onward	WALL-E
Good Dinosaur, The	Ratatouille	

WORDS IN THE FIRST VERSE
OF 'GOD SAVE THE QUEEN'

(Don't give them too long on this one)

And	Long	Send
Glorious	Noble	The
God	Our	To
Gracious	Over	Us
Happy	Queen	Victorious
Her	Reign	
Live	Save	

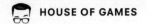

TITLES OF BOOKS IN THE MR. MEN SERIES

(Not including bespoke and tie-in one-offs)

Mr. Adventure	Mr. Good	Mr. Perfect
Mr. Bounce	Mr. Greedy	Mr. Quiet
Mr. Brave	Mr. Grumble	Mr. Rude
Mr. Bump	Mr. Grumpy	Mr. Rush
Mr. Busy	Mr. Happy	Mr. Silly
Mr. Calm	Mr. Impossible	Mr. Skinny
Mr. Chatterbox	Mr. Jelly	Mr. Slow
Mr. Cheerful	Mr. Lazy	Mr. Small
Mr. Christmas	Mr. Marvellous	Mr. Sneeze
Mr. Clever	Mr. Mean	Mr. Snow
Mr. Clumsy	Mr. Messy	Mr. Strong
Mr. Cool	Mr. Mischief	Mr. Tall
Mr. Daydream	Mr. Muddle	Mr. Tickle
Mr. Dizzy	Mr. Nobody	Mr. Topsy-Turvy
Mr. Forgetful	Mr. Noisy	Mr. Uppity
Mr. Funny	Mr. Nonsense	Mr. Worry
Mr. Fussy	Mr. Nosey	Mr. Wrong

EU CAPITAL CITIES

Amsterdam

Athens

Berlin

Bratislava

Brussels

Bucharest

Budapest

Copenhagen

Dublin

Helsinki

Lisbon

Ljubljana

Luxembourg

Madrid

Nicosia

Paris

Prague

Riga

Rome

Sofia

Stockholm

Tallinn

Valletta

Vienna

Vilnius

Warsaw

Zagreb (the winning answer; also the most *recent* capital at time of writing!)

ANSWERS

GAME 5: THE ANSWERS IN THE QUESTION
Part One
1. Dungarees
2. Mothering Sunday
3. Maurice Sendak
4. Sou'wester
5. *Murder on the Orient Express*

Part Two
1. Che Guevara
2. Claude Monet
3. Daley Thompson
4. Hairy Bikers
5. Aesop

GAME 7: BROKEN KARAOKE
1. 'She Loves You'
2. 'Ooh Aah ... Just a Little Bit'
3. 'I'd Do Anything for Love (But I Won't Do That)'
4. 'Wonderwall'
5. 'Baby Shark'*

---

* If you're remembering the fact from the previous *House of Games* book about this song's origins going back to a 1970s campfire version of the Jaws theme, we've used the date here of the appearance of the song in its current - some would say perfect - form.

SET 2 SCORECARD				
	Player 1	Player 2	Player 3	Player 4
Game 5				
Game 6				
Game 7				
Game 8				
Totals				

WINNER!

SET 3

... for which you need to
perfect a bluesy holler

GAME 9
LEAVE THIS WITH ME

You need: nothing

Players: pairs (plus someone to read the challenges if you're odd, as in an odd number)

Scoring: see below

Welcome to the House of Games Psych Lab, where we measure, in a unit known as the *frisson*, the experiences of pairs games; our aim is to find those which generate results in the Goldilocks zone of 'very mild to mild' discomfiture.

Here's an example. **The older contestant in each pair chooses whether to take the 1-point part of each question** (and risk looking cocky) **or the 2-point part** (and risk looking cowardly).

Once each pair has had a go, you can proceed with the younger contestant choosing.

1. *1 point:* London's Eurostar station

   2 points: Paris's Eurostar station

2. *1 point:* Medical name for the thigh bone

   2 points: Medical name for the buttocks

3. *1 point:* U2's lead singer

   2 points: U2's drummer

4. *1 point:* Istanbul's country

   2 points: Capital of Istanbul's country

5. *1 point:* Company that bought YouTube in 2006

   2 points: Parent company since 2015 of the company that bought YouTube in 2006

6. *1 point:* 1994 romcom with song 'Love Is All Around'

   2 points: Band with 1967 original version of 'Love Is All Around'

ANSWERS
See page 58

GAME 10

I'VE GOT THOSE HISTORICAL BLUES

You need: phone/tablet etc. to play a karaoke vid

Players: take it in turns to sing

Scoring: 3 points per answer

No-one who witnessed David O'Doherty in our *Games Night* episodes hollering bluesy clues to historical questions has managed to forget the incident. Not least the British Consortium of Blues Musicians, whose legal team inexplicably persuaded our Corporate Affairs department to sign an agreement preventing David from performing in the 12-bar format, anywhere in the known universe, in perpetuity.

This ban does not cover you though, dear reader. So **get up a karaoke video of Elvis doing 'Trouble', sing along and enjoy. First person to name the historical figure gets the 3 points each time.**

For maximum pleasure, all guesses should be (a) sung; (b) with gusto; (c) in the format 'I've got those [name of person] blues'.

1. Woke up this mornin'

    1605

    By January '06

    I won't even be alive

    Rented a cellar

    My mind set on slaughter

    Gon' be caught red-handed then hanged, drawn and quartered

    I've got the blues ...

2. Woke up this mornin'

    1936

    My woman has put me

    In a helluva fix

    Prime Minister Baldwin

    Says I should send her away

    But if I let my brother take my job I can marry that divorcée

    I've got the blues ...

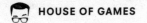

3. Woke up this mornin'

    44 BC

    I've fought Gaul and Britain

    And July's named 'cause of me

    I travelled here to the Senate

    Saw Brutus lookin' harsh

    I should have been more careful on those fateful Ides of March

    I got the blues …

4. Woke up this mornin'

    1903

    Kitty Hawk California

    Somewhere way way below me

    My brother and I flipped a coin

    To decide who'd be in the seat

    I was only up there for 12 seconds but it was a terrifying feat

    We've got the blues …

5.   Woke up this mornin'

1996

Surrounded by men in white coats

Who got mad genetics tricks

Scotland's Roslin Institute

Is where y'all find me

I never had no farmyard mother, just the boffins who designed me

I've got the blues ...

6.   Woke up this mornin'

1649

They say I'm guilty of treason

It's the end of the line

I know that swine Cromwell

I know where this is headed

They'll take me outside the Banqueting House and there I'll be beheaded

I've got the blues ...

7. Woke up this mornin'

1651

Parliamentary soldiers

Got me on the run

That no-good Cromwell

He wants to see me croak

So while the New Model Army rampages by I'll stay right here in this oak

I've got the blues ...

ANSWERS
See page 58

GAME 11
SIZE MATTERS

In this game, **we give you a category and everyone writes down something they think is in that category.** Cover up the possible answers.

You get 2 points if you've written the longest correct answer of all the guesses (count letters but not spaces, punctuation, etc.).

And you get 4 points if you've managed to find the **longest** of all the possible answers. We've listed them in order of bigness.

MONTHS OF THE YEAR
... in French

Septembre	Janvier	Août
Décembre	Juillet	Juin
Novembre	Octobre	Mars
Février	Avril	Mai

WINNERS OF *I'M A CELEB*

... up to Danny Miller, whose name is not very long

Christopher Biggins	Vicky Pattison
Giovanna Fletcher	Carl Fogarty
Jacqueline Jossa	Danny Miller
Scarlett Moffatt	Gino D'Acampo
Georgia Toffolo	Joe Pasquale
Carol Thatcher	Kerry Katona
Charlie Brooks	Phil Tufnell
Dougie Poynter	Matt Willis
Harry Redknapp	Joe Swash
Stacey Solomon	Kian Egan
Tony Blackburn	

ROALD DAHL CHILDREN'S NOVELS
... post-1960, no anthologies
or verse collections

Charlie and the Great Glass Elevator

Charlie and the Chocolate Factory

Danny, the Champion of the World

The Giraffe and the Pelly and Me

George's Marvellous Medicine

The Vicar of Nibbleswicke

James and the Giant Peach

The Enormous Crocodile

Fantastic Mr Fox

The Magic Finger

The Minpins

The Witches

Esio Trot

The Twits

Matilda

The BFG

AUSTRALIAN STATES AND TERRITORIES

... as listed in the *CIA World Factbook*

Australian Capital Territory

Northern Territory

Western Australia

South Australia

New South Wales

Queensland

Tasmania

Victoria

GAME 12

LOOK WHO'S BACK

You need: nothing extra

Players: any number

Scoring: 3 points per correct answer

There's a stark difference between the House of Games's entrance and its exit. Guests arrive in the Grand Vestibule where they are offered a choice of waters* before being escorted to Hair and Make-Up.**

At the *end* of the week, the tone changes. Guests are detained in the Holding Bay where they are expected to pay their way by contributing some questions for future episodes.

Below are the 'sample questions' we hand out, to point them in the right direction. **Take it in turns to pose them to each other.**

---

*   Admittedly, the choice is 'hot or cold tap'.
**   Until 2020, since when it's very much been 'bring your own comb'.

ANGELA BARNES

Angela was born on 9 November 1976. What symbol of oppression was destroyed on her 13th birthday?

ALEX HORNE

Alex loves all the instruments of the orchestra, especially the one that would be at least 12 feet long if straightened out. What's it called?

JEAN JOHANSSON

A Place in the Sun has taken Jean to all manner of Spain's Costas. Of the ten major Costas, can you name three?

VALERIE SINGLETON

In 1971, Valerie toured Kenya with HRH Princess Anne, because the princess had just taken on what role?

GYLES BRANDRETH

In 1817, what happened to Giles's forebear, Jeremiah Brandreth?

ANSWERS

See page 58

ANSWERS

GAME 9: LEAVE THIS WITH ME

1. St Pancras International; Gare du Nord
2. Femur; Nates
3. Bono; Larry Mullen Jr
4. Turkey; Ankara
5. Alphabet; Google
6. *Four Weddings and a Funeral*; The Troggs

GAME 10: I'VE GOT THOSE HISTORICAL BLUES

1. I've got those Guy Fawkes blues
2. I've got those Edward VIII blues
3. I've got those Julius Caesar blues
4. We've got those Wright Brothers blues
5. I've got those Dolly the Cloned Sheep blues
6. I've got those Charles I blues
7. I've got those Charles II blues

GAME 12: LOOK WHO'S BACK

Angela: The Berlin Wall

Alex: The French Horn

Jean: Costa del Sol, Costa Brava, Costa Blanca, Costa Cálida, Costa de Almería, Costa Tropical, Costa de la Luz, Costa Dorada, Costa del Azahar, Costa Verde

Valerie: President of Save the Children

Gyles: He was beheaded (with an axe, for treason)

SET 3 SCORECARD			
	Player 1	Player 2	Player 3	Player 4
Game 9				
Game 10				
Game 11				
Game 12				
Totals				

WINNER!

SET 4

... in which you might
consider your life choices

GAME 13
MOUSE OF GAMES

Anything you have read about a secret room in the House of Games where we are training super-intelligent rodents to enjoy quizzes is just silly hearsay. Even if we *were* doing that, the conditions for the mice would be beyond humane. Luxurious, even. Apropos of nothing, I'll escort you straight past *that* door and change the subject.

Choose one of the categories. An opposing player will read you a description of a TV show, poem, etc. It is entirely made-up, but **it is also a real TV show, poem, etc. *with one letter changed***. So if the description of an artist was 'Spanish surrealist who sells ham and cheese', you would answer not 'Salvador Dalí', but 'Salvador Deli'.

Thinking of cheese ...

TYPES OF CHEESE

1. This salty Greek cheese is often served at summer fairs.

2. This soft white French cheese has a lively, vigorous spirit.

3. You can enjoy this red-rinded Dutch cheese if you get enough questions correct in a formal test.

4. This English blue cheese was actually invented by a former England goalkeeper.

5. This Indian cheese is best enjoyed while driving a German tank.

WIMBLEDON SINGLES CHAMPIONS

1. In the 1980s, this blond German champion enjoyed his barley water from a plastic sippy cup.

2. This three-named American champion of the 1960s and 1970s is also the sister of Chandler from *Friends*.

3. This left-handed Spanish champion speaks in a pinched, adenoidal tone.

4. This Australian champion won the men's singles in 1987 and celebrated with his favourite creamy potato dish.

5. Known as the Swiss Miss, this champion is also a carpenter who will gladly mend your wobbly door.

ANSWERS
See page 74

GAME 14
POP ART

You need: this book and a little lateral thinking

Players: any number

Scoring: 10 points if you get it from the words describing the song, then the points available go down by 2 for every image you reveal.

This round requires you: (a) to operate a complicated kit of technical equipment also known as 'two sheets of paper'; (b) to be patient and above all honest.

On the next few pages, you will see four collections of four images. **Each collection depicts a well-known song.** Start with both pieces of paper covering both pages in each opening. Reveal the images one at a time.

Yell out randomly as many times as you like. You are *not* frozen out for wrong guesses and we are looking for titles only.

SONG 1

1969, classic pop

CLUE: England terrace favourite of the Euros in 2021

SONG 2

1981, synthpop

CLUE: Classic 'he said, she said' breakup song

SONG 3

1990, Madchester

CLUE: The vocalist also called his autobiography
Twisting My Melon

SONG 4

1958, crooner's standard

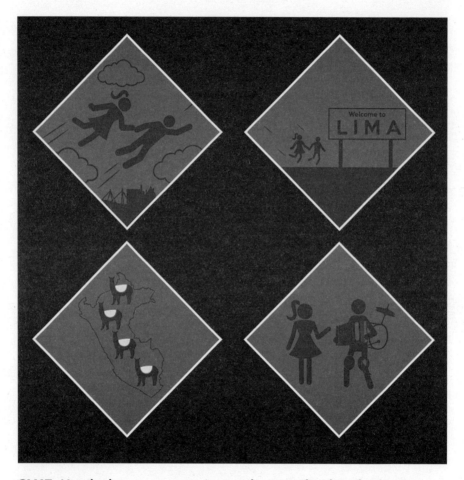

CLUE: Used whenever a movie needs to evoke the glamorous age of jet travel

ANSWERS
See page 74

GAME 15
20,8,5 3,15,4,5 7,1,13,5

You need: nothing else

Players: 2 or more

Scoring: 2 points for the first person to
shout each correct answer

Hang on to a piece of paper from the previous game, because you'll
again be blocking as you go.

We're going to show you a category, then some things in that
category, with every letter replaced with a number. In this code, 'A's
become '1's. 'B's become '2's. 'C's become '3's. 'D's ... you may have
cracked the algorithm.

**Move the piece of paper to reveal each line of code, then confirm
the answers as needed.**

If you don't have buzzers, just howl in each other's ears.

UK CITIES

12,5,5,4,19

5,4,9,14,2,21,18,7,8

4,5,18,2,25

16,5,20,5,18,2,15,18,15,21,7,8

2,1,20,8

CLASSIC 1980S MOVIES

23,8,5,14 8,1,18,18,25 13,5,20 19,1,12,12,25

4,9,18,20,25 4,1,14,3,9,14,7

6,15,15,20,12,15,15,19,5

20,8,5 7,15,15,14,9,5,19

2,9,7

TENNIS TERMS

12,5,20

1,4,22,1,14,20,1,7,5

2,1,3,11,8,1,14,4

22,15,12,12,5,25

6,1,13,5 19,5,20 1,14,4 13,1,20,3,8

ON THE TAKEAWAY MENU

3,15,4

3,8,9,16,19

3,21,18,18,25 19,1,21,3,5

6,9,19,8,3,1,11,5

2,1,20,20,5,18,5,4 19,1,21,19,1,7,5

ANSWERS
See page 74

GAME 16
CAN YOU FEEL IT?

You need: the items specified below plus pillowcase, pencil, paper and phone-as-stopwatch

Players: any number

Scoring: 2 points per item identified

The home version of this game is somewhat different.

If you wish to replicate the TV version, we can't stop you. All you need is a small (approx. A5-size) whiteboard per player and a set of magnetic letters. Start each player with the same word and give them clues for answers that can be made from the letters in the starting word. Try to keep a good mix of subjects with short answers and keep going until the whole messy process becomes unbearable – at least, that's what we did here in the House of Games.

Your version is simpler. **Give each player pencil, paper and a pillowcase containing the following items. In turn, each has two minutes to identify as many as they can by touch alone.**

a lateral-flow test

just the ring of a keyring

an obsolete SIM card from an old phone

whatever you used to spring open the SIM card section

the most specialised item in your kitchen drawer, be that a prawn de-veiner or, more likely, something like a measuring spoon

cap of a toothpaste tube

half a facemask

a grain of your choosing, anywhere on the scale from easy-cook rice to quinoa

a silica gel sachet

an arcane bit of kit that someone in your household uses to tune or otherwise tend to a musical instrument; if no-one in your household plays a musical instrument, for heaven's sake make some life changes and just use a pebble or something for now

ANSWERS

GAME 13: MOUSE OF GAMES

Types of Cheese

1. Fete
2. Brio
3. Exam
4. Shilton
5. Panzer

Wimbledon Singles Champions

1. Boris Beaker
2. Billie Jean Bing
3. Rafael Nasal
4. Pat Mash
5. Martina Hinges

GAME 14: POP ART

SONG 1: 'Sweet Caroline'

SONG 2: 'Don't You Want Me'

SONG 3: 'Step On'

SONG 4: 'Come Fly with Me'

GAME 15: 20,8,5 3,15,4,5 7,1,13,5

UK CITIES

12,5,5,4,19 – Leeds

5,4,9,14,2,21,18,7,8 – Edinburgh

4,5,18,2,25 – Derby

16,5,20,5,18,2,15,18,15,21,7,8
    – Peterborough

2,1,20,8 – Bath

CLASSIC 1980s MOVIES

23,8,5,14 8,1,18,18,25 13,5,20
    19,1,12,12,25 – *When Harry Met Sally*

4,9,18,20,25 4,1,14,3,9,14,7
    – *Dirty Dancing*

6,15,15,20,12,15,15,19,5 – *Footloose*

20,8,5 7,15,15,14,9,5,19 – *The Goonies*

2,9,7 – *Big*

TENNIS TERMS

12,5,20 – Let

1,4,22,1,14,20,1,7,5 – Advantage

2,1,3,11,8,1,14,4 – Backhand

22,15,12,12,5,25 – Volley

6,1,13,5 19,5,20 1,14,4 13,1,20,3,8
    – Game, set and match

ON THE TAKEAWAY MENU

3,15,4 – Cod

3,8,9,16,19 – Chips

3,21,18,18,25 19,1,21,3,5 – Curry sauce

6,9,19,8,3,1,11,5 – Fishcake

2,1,20,20,5,18,5,4 19,1,21,19,1,7,5
    – Battered sausage

SET 4 SCORECARD			
	Player 1	Player 2	Player 3	Player 4
Game 13				
Game 14				
Game 15				
Game 16				
Totals				

WINNER!

SET 5

... in which you will despair at the choices made by car-buyers

GAME 17
SEE MY GUESTS

You'll see two images of guests from the TV version of *House of Games*. If you can tell who they are straightaway, that's *10 points each*. (Get someone else to check, in case you're wrong.)

If you can't, then there are some questions underneath, of the kind we use in our round It's All In The Name. As that name suggests, this will give you some of the letters of the guest's name. But each time you use one of these questions, the points available go down by 2.

Cooperation and inspiration: and you'll all boost your scores.

GUEST ONE

For 10 points:

    Can you name them?

Answer these questions to get some of the letters in their name.

For 8 points:

    Delicious cold pudding of cream beaten with sugar, wine
    and lemon juice

For 6 points:

    Chocolaty wood-shaped festive concoction

For 4 points:

    Complete the Bob Dylan song title: 'It's All Over Now …'

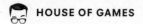
For 2 points:

> Bird which steals your chips at the beach

GUEST TWO

For 10 points:

> Can you name them?

Answer these questions to get some of the letters in their name.

For 8 points:

> Your biggest internal organ

For 6 points:

> Location of the Reina Sofía Museum and the Prado

For 4 points:

Musical instrument with a keyboard whose name is French for 'keyboard'

For 2 points:

Fictional species of Disney's Ariel

ANSWERS
See page 88

GAME 18
YOU COMPLETE ME

You need: buzzers or some kind of noise-makers

Players: 4 (plus someone to read things out)

Scoring: 2 points for every correct answer

Get into pairs. If no-one wants to go with you, sorry, and you're the one reading on.

All the answers have two words. **Whoever buzzes first can only give the first word - and their partner earns each of them 2 points *only* if they can successfully also give the *second* word.**

(If they don't, you can pass it over - and don't let on if the first word was wrong: keep things exciting even if there are no points at stake.)

1.   When telling the time, what does 'AM' stand for?

2.   What is the name of the world's tallest building?

3.   How many years were there between England winning the World Cup and London next hosting the Olympics?

4.   Which 1997 film starring Colin Firth as an obsessive football fan has a 2005 US remake that switches the sport for baseball?

5. Which Russian revolutionary founded the Bolshevik party and became the first leader of the Soviet state?

6. In which Victorian farce does Lord Fancourt Babberley impersonate a friend's female relative?

7. In Australia and New Zealand, what name is given to 25 April, which marks a remembrance of veterans?

8. In *The Simpsons*, who is Mr Burns's assistant?

9. Belmont FC was the original name of which club based in Birkenhead?

10. In which film does Jim Carrey play a lawyer who discovers he cannot say anything dishonest?

ANSWERS

See page 88

GAME 19
WIN WHEN THEY'RE SINGING

You need: phone/tablet/laptop each (plus one more)
Players: any number
Scoring: 3 points for the closest each time

Come on in to the Music Library. We tend to prefer songs that have a lot of information, ideally formatted in some kind of list. 'We Didn't Start the Fire', great. Fleetwood Mac's 'Albatross', not so much. 'It's The End of the World as We Know It (And I Feel Fine)', yes please. Classical and jazz, think again.

For quizzing purposes, however, we're prepared to stray outside our comfort zone. This game involves six songs with intros you should recognise instantly.

One contestant should get the song up, skip any ads, then count down 'three, two one' and press play. At that point, everyone presses START on their stopwatch app.

The song should be muted after two or three seconds, but **the stopwatches carry on until the moment you think the vocals kick in**, when you press STOP.

Once everyone has stopped, restart the song and see who was nearest.

1. Abba, 'SOS'

2. Joni Mitchell, 'Big Yellow Taxi'

3. Sister Sledge, 'He's the Greatest Dancer'

4. Irene Cara, 'Flashdance … What a Feeling'

5. Mark Ronson feat. Bruno Mars, 'Uptown Funk'

6. Guns N' Roses, 'Sweet Child o' Mine'

GAME 20
FIVES ALIVES

You need: nothing

Players: any number

Scoring: work together and then divvy up 20 points on merit

Let's now go to Richard's Study. It's a simple room, as you'd expect: a tidy writing desk, some reference works, a bath of sheep's milk and some notebooks. And in one of those notebooks, notes on a game Richard devised named Fives Alives. **You're given the initials of the Top Five in some category, and you fill in the rest.**

A) COUNTRIES WITH THE MOST DOGS

5 J

4 R

3 C

2 B

1 A

B) MOST DOWNLOADED APPS OF 2021

5 T

4 W

3 F

2 I

1 T

C) BRITAIN'S MOST POPULAR PUDDINGS

5 C

4 J

3 CC

2 VS

1 AC

D) UK'S MOST COMMON COLOUR OF NEW CARS

5 R

4 B

3 W

2 B

1 G

ANSWERS

See page 88

ANSWERS

GAME 17: SEE MY GUESTS

GUEST ONE

For 8 points: Syllabub

For 6 points: Yule log

For 4 points: 'Baby Blue'

For 2 points: Seagull

Answer: Bobby Seagull

GUEST TWO

For 8 points: Liver

For 6 points: Madrid

For 4 points: Clavier

For 2 points: Mermaid

Answer: Val McDermid

GAME 18: YOU COMPLETE ME

1. Ante meridiem
2. Burj Khalifa
3. Forty-six
4. *Fever Pitch*
5. Vladimir Lenin
6. *Charley's Aunt*
7. Anzac Day
8. Waylon Smithers
9. Tranmere Rovers
10. *Liar Liar*

GAME 20: FIVES ALIVES

A) Japan, Russia, China, Brazil, America

B) Telegram, WhatsApp, Facebook, Instagram, TikTok

C) Cheesecake, jelly, carrot cake, Victoria sponge, apple crumble

D) Red, blue, white, black, grey

SET 5 SCORECARD

	Player 1	Player 2	Player 3	Player 4
Game 17				
Game 18				
Game 19				
Game 20				
Totals				

WINNER!

SET 6

... for which you must remember
to use the *cold* tap

GAME 21
NOT RHYME TIME

You need: nothing extra

Players: any number, plus 1 to read out the questions

Scoring: 5 points per correct answer

This game is not Rhyme Time. It is, instead, Not Rhyme Time. In Rhyme Time, the answers rhyme. The clues do not.

In Not Rhyme Time, **the clue contains something that rhymes with the answer.** One person should read them out in a pleasing rhythm and everyone else gets to shout their guesses. Incorrect guessers are *not* frozen out.

1. Of this sitcom's large cast

    Our favourite is Jones

    Who's often thrown into alarm – he

    Also likes saying

    'They don't like it up 'em!'

    And the name of the show is …

2. Back in the eighties,

   In Britain in winter

   This sport enjoyed bigger ratings

   When Torvill and Dean

   Burst onto the scene

   And wowed us with their ...

3. If you love indie,

   You'll be cock-a-hoop

   'Cause you won't find this question so tricky

   We need the name of

   Lauren Laverne's group

   Who sang 'Punka': and that name was ...

4. When your emails come

   From phone to computer

   There's kit that you need to decode 'em

   Its full name is

   Modulator-demodulator

   But it's usually known as a ...

ANSWERS
See page 100

GAME 22
TENSE SQUIRTERS

You need: a squirter (see below)

Players: 3 or more

Scoring: 10 points for whoever is driest at the end,
to be agreed by popular vote or argument;
5 each for the next least damp

You enjoyed the Tense Water Pistol Game in the previous *House of Games* book, so it's back. With a new name. I mean, weaponry? In a family book? Based on a cosy teatime telly quiz? Dear me, no. What were we thinking? It was a different time, and attitudes have changed. So grab yourself a non-military squirter - be it seahorse, mermaid or bloater - and get tense.

When it's your turn to hold the squirter, take a look at the list of categories below. Choose one and read it out, then secretly write down something that fits that category.

Now, go round the other players in turn. Aim the squirter at their face and ask them to name something in that category. If it's not what you wrote down, they're safe (for now) and you move on to the next player.

But: don't move on too quickly. They might blurt out an answer quickly, but you can take your time. Make them wait. Fix their gaze. Make them sweat. Enjoy yourself.

And, of course, when someone *does* say what you wrote down, let them have it. Both barrels. Don't hold back. Because they won't when it's their turn - which is now.

CATEGORIES

Countries beginning with 'S'

Salad ingredients

Sitcoms

Numbers under 30

Everyday items of clothing

People who live near you

BBC radio stations

Fairy tales

… or add your own. For extra tension, play the same category repeatedly as a test of memory and nerve.

GAME 23
CINE-NYMS

You need: just this book

Players: any number, plus someone to read the clues

Scoring: 4 points per correct answer

Welcome to the House of Games's most cinematic space, the Screening Room. There's no point coming in the afternoons, as the question producers Tom and Abby have block-booked it for the foreseeable future for a daily viewing of *Cool Runnings*. In the mornings, though, we watch some classic movies and come up with interesting rewritings of their most recognisable lines.

Which films do the following paraphrased lines come from? Just the movie title each time please.

1. 'Around four grams of simple carbohydrates will assist ingestion of the pharmaceutical.'

2. 'I'm not atrocious, I'm simply illustrated in a manner that suggests such.'

3. 'At an indefinite future time, genuine precipitation will arrive, and clean this unpleasant material from the byways.'

4.   'Care to construct a humanoid from hard water flakes?'

5.   'Large error. Large. Gigantic.'

ANSWERS
See page 100

GAME 24

DISTINCTLY AVERAGE

You need: pencil and paper; a phone, or someone who's good with numbers

Players: 4, 6, 8, 10 ... basically, an even number that's 4 or more

Scoring: 4 points for every win

You know the drill. Get into pairs. You'll be given a question to which you can only guess the answer. **You and your partner will then take the average of your guesses. The pair that's closest to the actual number gets the points.** You will then lambast your partner for skewing the average away from your perfectly good guess ... unless, of course, the lambasting is rightfully yours.

1. How many takeaway shops and mobile food stands are there in the UK?

2. What is the total length in miles of the South West Coast Path, the UK's longest National Trail?

3. Lasting 29 minutes, how many shots were played in the longest rally in professional tennis?

4. In pounds, how much did singer Kelly Clarkson pay for a ring that once belonged to Jane Austen?

5. How many hemisemidemiquavers are there in a single 4:4 bar?

ANSWERS

See page 100

ANSWERS

GAME 21: NOT RHYME TIME

1. *Dad's Army*
2. Figure skating
3. Kenickie
4. Modem

GAME 23: CINE-NYMS

1. *Mary Poppins* ('A spoonful of sugar helps the medicine go down.')
2. *Who Framed Roger Rabbit* ('I'm not bad; I'm just drawn that way.')
3. *Taxi Driver* ('Someday a real rain will come and wash all this scum off the streets.')
4. *Frozen* ('Do you wanna build a snowman?')
5. *Pretty Woman* ('Big mistake. Big. Huge!')

GAME 24: DISTINCTLY AVERAGE

1. 37,465
2. 630
3. 643
4. 152,450
5. 64

SET 6 SCORECARD			
	Player 1	Player 2	Player 3	Player 4
Game 21				
Game 22				
Game 23				
Game 24				
Totals				

WINNER!

SET 7

... in which you may discover if your relatives operate a burner phone

GAME 25
WRONG YOU ARE

You need: a fork and a spoon for each player

Players: any number, plus someone to read the questions

Scoring: 2 points per incorrect answer

Welcome to the Gameplay Testing Room, where we invite civilians to answer questions in a game we're trying out. Thank you for joining us. After you've signed this baffling and lengthy non-disclosure agreement, we can begin. You don't need to read the agreement, it's fine: just sign.

OK, in Wrong You Are, someone will read you a clue and then an answer for Fork and an answer for Spoon. **You then have three seconds (they'll count you down) to bang the wrong item of cutlery on the table. Wrong answers only, in terms of points.**

Person reading the questions: (a) we've put an arrow next to the answer that gets the points; (b) feel free to make the '3-2-1' countdown quite oppressive.

1. What is the capital of Australia?

   FORK: Sydney «

   SPOON: Canberra

2. What football team do the Gallagher brothers support?

   FORK: Manchester United «

   SPOON: Manchester City

3. Which of these monarchs reigned for less time?

   FORK: Lady Jane Grey

   SPOON: Queen Victoria «

4. What's the middle colour of the rainbow?

   FORK: Blue «

   SPOON: Green

5. Which Spice Girl was known as Scary?

   FORK: Mel B

   SPOON: Mel C «

6. Which is not a Sylvester Stallone role?

   FORK: Rocky

   SPOON: Bullwinkle «

7. What's half of a perfect darts score?

   FORK: 90

   SPOON: 180 «

8. What nationality was Hercule Poirot's creator?

   FORK: Belgian «

   SPOON: English

GAME 26
THE Z LIST

As before, **you get 1 point if your answer fits the category,
3 points if yours is the last alphabetically of everyone playing and
5 points if yours is the answer that comes last alphabetically of
all the acceptable answers that we kindly provide.** Cover up the
possible answers.

Ignore, please, any 'The's, 'A's etc. at the beginning of possible
answers. That's standard.

MADONNA NUMBER ONE SINGLES

'American Pie'

'Frozen'

'Hung Up'

'Into the Groove'

'La Isla Bonita'

'Like a Prayer'

'Music'

'Papa Don't Preach'

'Sorry'

'True Blue'

'Vogue'

'Who's That Girl'

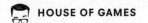
ENGINES OF REV. W. AWDRY'S RAILWAY SERIES

(just the first names of the North Western Railway Steam Engines, and not the '... the Wicked Engine' part)

Donald	Gordon	Percy
Douglas	Henry	Thomas
Duck	James	Toby
Edward	Oliver	

OFFICIAL LANGUAGES OF THE EUROPEAN UNION

Bulgarian	French	Maltese
Croatian	German	Polish
Czech	Greek	Portuguese
Danish	Hungarian	Romanian
Dutch	Irish	Slovak
English	Italian	Slovenian
Estonian	Latvian	Spanish
Finnish	Lithuanian	Swedish

GREAT-GRANDCHILDREN OF QUEEN ELIZABETH II

Archie	Isla	Lucas
August	Lena	Mia
Charlotte	Lilibet	Savannah
George	Louis	Sienna

GAME 27
IS/WAS

You need: just yourselves and us

Players: an even number, it's a pairs game

Scoring: 2 points per correct question;
bonus point if both halves answered correctly

Arrange yourself into pairs. If you're an odd number, the odd person can ask the questions.

Ask the questions one at a time, the first to the person on the left; the second to the person on the right.

1. Who is the presenter of the BBC quiz *A Question of Sport*?

    Who *was* the *previous* presenter of the BBC quiz *A Question of Sport*?

2. What is the name of India's most populous city?

    What *was* the name of India's most populous city until 1995?

3. Who plays M to Daniel Craig's Bond?

    Who *used to* play M to Daniel Craig's Bond?

4. What is the name of the Sussex town visited by George V for a health cure in 1929?

    Before his visit, what *was* the name of the Sussex town visited by George V for a health cure in 1929?

5. In the BBC sitcom *Still Open All Hours*, who is the proprietor of the corner shop where much of the comic action is set?

    In the BBC sitcom *Open All Hours*, who *was* the proprietor of the corner shop where much of the comic action was set?

6. How many zeroes are there in an official British billion?

    How many zeroes *were* there in a British billion in the 1960s?

ANSWERS

See page 114

GAME 28
THINK LIKE A QUESTION SETTER

You need: a smartphone or tablet for each player; something to block off parts of the page

Players: 2 or more

Scoring: 5 points for anyone who recovers access to their device

This is the game that caused the biggest kerfuffle when the previous *House of Games* book was published. There was resentment, there were recriminations and in the case of Mrs B. Lewis of South Wittering, we can only apologise that you missed your daughter's wedding. As a token of our kindness (a token which does not accept any legal liability for your very obvious distress) we have mailed you a collection of unclaimed prizes. (Pro tip: unless you've got a full set of current inoculations, do *not* allow the *House of Games* sarong to come into contact with bare skin.)

Here's how to play.

Unlock your phone or tablet and go to the Password option in Settings. Disable recognition by face/thumbprint, etc. Get the device ready to receive a new numeric passcode.

Pass your device to the player on your left (swap if there are two of you, duh).

When it's your turn, use your House of Games Spoiler Blocker™ (otherwise known as a blank piece of paper) to reveal one of the Answer Sets below. Choose enough answers to create a new passcode, then enter it into the device you have been passed. Confirm the new passcode. (WRITE IT DOWN AS WELL in case you forget what you've chosen.)

Now pass the device back to its owner and give them the clues in the right order.

If they fail to regain access after two attempts, they must find out the answers using pre-phone technology. Welcome to how we used to live.

ANSWER SET ONE

Two to the power six: 64

Shirt number worn by Drogba, Giggs, Romário and Best: 11

Number of legs in 12 standard octopuses: 96

ANSWER SET TWO

Square root of 256: 16

Number between 3 and 7 on a dartboard: 19

Number of spaces on two Monopoly boards: 80

ANSWER SET THREE

Three to the power four: 81

Number of players on eight volleyball courts: 96

Number of pawns in three chess sets: 48

ANSWER SET FOUR

Square root of 169: 13

Width in metres of Olympic swimming pool: 25

Number of strings on 28 balalaikas: 84

ANSWERS

GAME 27: IS/WAS

1. Paddy McGuinness; Sue Barker
2. Mumbai; Bombay
3. Ralph Fiennes; Judi Dench
4. Bognor Regis; Bognor
5. Granville; Arkwright
6. 9; 12

SET 7 SCORECARD			
	Player 1	Player 2	Player 3	Player 4
Game 25				
Game 26				
Game 27				
Game 28				
Totals				

WINNER!

SET 8

... in which you will strive to
be a plausible cockney

GAME 29
POP ART

You need: this book and some paper

Players: any number

Scoring: 10 points if you get it from the words describing the song, then the points available go down by 2 for every image you reveal

OK, get some sheets of paper ready so that you see the clues one at a time. (Or you could cover the clues with a quiz book from some other TV show, one where they've lovelessly pasted in questions that have already been broadcast.)

Then gather round.

On the next few pages, you will see four collections of three or four images. **Each collection depicts a well-known song.** Start with both pieces of paper covering both pages in each opening. Reveal the images one at a time.

Yell out randomly as many times as you like. You are *not* frozen out for wrong guesses and we are looking for titles only.

SONG 1

1978, disco floor-filler

CLUE: Gloria's biggest hit by far

SONG 2

1990, pop-rap

CLUE: Performer's large trousers not pictured

SONG 3

2003, stadium indie

CLUE: His surname really is Flowers

SONG 4

1967, soul evergreen

CLUE: Not pictured: amazing stacks of 'together's and 'forever's in the chorus

ANSWERS

See page 129

GAME 30
HIDDEN IN PLAIN SIGHT

You need: just a friendly attitude

Players: any number

Scoring: 3 points per answer

We can do this the nice way or the other way.

The nice way involves you gathering around the clues and working together to **find the answer, which is literally hidden in the text.** For example, the phrase 'You might use this sauce in a delicious **oy**ster stir-fry' both describes soy and contains the word 'soy'. We won't put the word in **bold type** in the real questions as that would turn the exercise from quizzing to merely reading.

The other way is the same, except you race to point to the bit of the sentence where the answer's hiding.

1. A hospitable inhabitant of Corfu might offer you this bread filled with tasty kofta.

2. At this Berkshire town's music festival, you may have to share a dingy tent.

3. This film shows you Paradise Falls from the veranda of a flying house.

4. If you were given this wriggling invertebrate in a Bushtucker Trial, you might quickly chew or munch slowly.

5. This football club was clever to nab a successful Italian manager in 2019.

6. For lunch in this capital city, many pick a bulgur-wheat dish known as *dalda*.

7. If you hit a team-mate with your mallet in this sport, apologise immediately.

8. This singer's band announced they would carbon offset the effects of their tour promoting the *No Line on the Horizon* album.

ANSWERS
See page 129

GAME 31
THE PEN-ULTIMATE ROUND

> **You need:** pencil and paper
> **Players:** at least 3
> **Scoring:** see below

Take it in turns to read out the titles below. **Everyone else writes down what they think is a plausible first sentence of the thing in question,** and you'll write out the real one, which we've provided at no extra cost.

Then read all the 'first sentences' in random order and ask the others which they think is genuine.

You get 1 point if anyone believes yours was the real McCoy.

1. *The Wind in the Willows* by Kenneth Grahame

    ('The mole had been working very hard all the morning, spring-cleaning his little home.')

2. **Meryl Streep's Best Actress Oscar acceptance speech, 1983**

    ('Oh, boy! No matter how much you try to imagine what this is like, it's just so incredibly thrilling, right down to your toes.')

3. *Frankenstein* **by Mary Shelley**

    ('You will rejoice to hear that no disaster has accompanied the commencement of an enterprise which you have regarded with such evil forebodings.')

4. **The first Poldark novel, by Winston Graham**

    ('It was windy.')

5. **The first episode of** *EastEnders*

    ('Stinks in 'ere.')

GAME 32
FIVE FOR THREE

You need: a phone

Players: any number

Scoring: 2 points each time you
get three answers out in time

In his medical book *Kay's Anatomy*, Adam Kay gently ridicules anyone who believes that bacteria might take as many as five seconds to get involved with a biscuit you've dropped on the floor. Let's just say that Adam's message has not reached all the question writers in the House of Games, to the extent that we have a special, unused and pristine Coffee Break Room ready for a visit from the great man, which we will pretend is how we normally live. In the meantime, our version (the Five-Day Rule) stands for biscuits, cakes and sweets. Longer for Haribo.

In this game, take turns. One player sets their phone's timer to five seconds, reads a category to another contestant and presses START. **If the other contestant can name three things in that category, they get a point.**

CATEGORIES

Countries beginning with 'I'

Popes

Berries that aren't strawberries or raspberries

The Masked Singer contestants

Oceans that aren't the Pacific or Atlantic

Chancellors of the Exchequer

Five-digit numbers that read the same backwards as forwards

Ford car marques

Inhabitants of the Marvel Comics Universe that you have just made up

Gases in the periodic table

Things in the home you are currently in that show the time

If the challenge is not sufficiently stiff, feel free to increase the quota to five. You will need to verify your own answers; we'd love to help but we can't do everything around here.

ANSWERS

GAME 29: POP ART

SONG 1: 'I Will Survive'

SONG 2: 'U Can't Touch This'

SONG 3: 'Mr Brightside'

SONG 4: 'I Say a Little Prayer'

GAME 30: HIDDEN IN PLAIN SIGHT

1. Pita
2. Reading
3. *Up*
4. Worm
5. Everton
6. Kabul
7. Polo
8. Bono

SET 8 SCORECARD			
	Player 1	Player 2	Player 3	Player 4
Game 29				
Game 30				
Game 31				
Game 32				
Totals				

WINNER!

SET 9

... in which only one person should read on following the words 'only one person should read on'

GAME 33
KLAUS OF GAMES

You need: nothing extra

Players: any number

Scoring: 2 points for each mangled title

Come now to the Mouse Annexe of the House of Games. We are now dealing with so many variants of the Mouse of Games family – change a letter, add a letter, remove a letter and another which we will encounter presently – that we built an extension to house them.

In case the name isn't clear enough (and please don't say it isn't – we don't want to reopen the debate over whether to call it Strauss of Games or indeed Laos of Games), this is the one where we give you synopses of films and TV shows where one word has been swapped for something that rhymes with it.

For example, if the clue were 'A shelled gastropod travels very slowly from Paris to London', you would answer not *A Tale of Two Cities* but *A Snail of Two Cities*.

Shall we?

UK TV SHOWS

1. After every round in Romesh Ranganathan's quiz show, the most humble and timid contestant is voted off.

2. Maître d' Fred and barman Merlin welcome singletons to their restaurant, but they are all doomed, hexed, jinxed I tells ya.

3. Four very different Scumbag College undergraduates are attacked by bees in their squalid house.

4. Martel Maxwell, Martin Roberts and Dion Dublin auction off bearded garden ornaments.

5. On this big-money quiz show, a fictional bear might phone his friend Piglet.

ROMCOM MOVIES

1. Tom Hanks and Meg Ryan walk around a city in Washington State trying to recover a military road vehicle.

2. Nia Vardalos deals with her boisterous family while planning to destroy a large quantity of paperwork.

3. Renée Zellweger plays a singleton looking for love in a building full of monks.

4. Hugh Grant woos Julia Roberts in a part of west London that's blighted by the stench of putrefaction.

5. Business rivals Tom Hanks and Meg Ryan unwittingly fall in love while sending each other small game birds.

ANSWERS
See page 146

GAME 34
WATCH YOUR BREATH

You need: self-control

Players: 2 or more

Scoring: see below

In this game, you might not know all the answers first time, but that shouldn't be an issue, as you'll see. The youngest player goes first.

Consider the first set. **Your job is to give all four answers in one go, without pausing or drawing breath.** If you don't manage it, play passes to the right. The first person to pull it off gets 5 points. Then move on to the next set.

When we play this among ourselves in the House of Games, whether that's in working hours to rigorously test a game, or to relax after rigorously testing games, people tend to 'game' the game by giving deliberately wrong answers until they're ready but we're sure you'll play it with a more collegiate spirit.

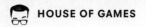

SET ONE

Played Jack Bauer in *24*

Hyacinth Bucket sitcom

Plays Black Widow in Avengers movies

Oasis follow-up album to *Definitely Maybe*

SET TWO

Lead actor in *Kindergarten Cop*

Alliterative rivals of West Bromwich Albion

George Lazenby's only Bond movie

Victor Meldrew sitcom

SET THREE

Author of *Little Women*

Hudson/McConaughey romcom based on dating 'don'ts'

2001 J. K. Rowling spin-off guide book

Princess Margaret in series three and four of *The Crown*

SET FOUR

1998 Vinnie Jones movie crime caper

Author of *The Great Gatsby*

Bombalurina novelty hit about beachwear

Annual BBC award usually won by Andy Murray

ANSWERS
See page 146

GAME 35
SEE MY GUESTS

You need: to block off parts of the following pages as you go

Players: any number (and someone to check your guesses)

Scoring: see below

You'll see two images of guests from the TV version of *House of Games*. If you can tell who they are straightaway, that's *10 points each*. (Get someone else to check, in case you're wrong.)

If you can't, then there are some nice straightforward questions underneath, of the kind we use in our round It's All In The Name. As that name suggests, this will give you some of the letters of the guest's name. But each time you use one of these questions, *the points available go down by 2*.

Cooperation and inspiration: and you'll all boost your scores.

GUEST ONE

For 10 points:

    Can you name them?

Answer these questions to get some of the letters in their name.

For 8 points:

    Types of energy like coal and gas

For 6 points:

    Navy-like shade associated with Queen Charlotte

For 4 points:

    Clothing-related term designating manual work

For 2 points:

First wife of Henry VIII to be beheaded

GUEST TWO

For 10 points:

Can you name them?

Answer these questions to get some of the letters in their name.

For 8 points:

Edmund who climbed Everest with Tenzing

For 6 points:

Creamy cake defined by Chambers Dictionary as being long (in terms of shape) and also short (in terms of duration)

For 4 points:

Davidson's childhood friend and motorcycle business partner

For 2 points:

S Club 7 song with a video featuring a pink bus that takes flight and heads for the stars

ANSWERS

See page 146

GAME 36

ONLY ONE PERSON SHOULD READ ON

This game has a slightly bossy name because it's important that only you, the one person who has read on, knows what's going to happen.

First of all, ask everyone else, possibly separately, to write down their best guesses for the following questions.

1. How many sledging dogs did Shackleton take with him to the Antarctic?

2. Which country won the celebrated ice hockey game known as 'The Miracle on Ice'?

3. How old was George Foreman when he regained the world heavyweight title in 1994?

4. Which act has the Guinness World Record for the longest same-pitch vocal note in a hit single?

Now get the following songs up on your phone. Announce the question number, press play and then pause just before the bit specified in brackets. Point to a player and get them to read out their answer.

1. Bryan Adams, 'Summer of '69' (69)

2. Bruce Springsteen, 'Born in the USA' (The USA)

3. Cornershop, 'Brimful of Asha' (45)

4. Abba, 'Knowing Me, Knowing You' (A-ha)

ANSWERS

GAME 33: KLAUS OF GAMES

UK TV Shows

1. *The Meekest Link*
2. *Cursed Dates*
3. *The Stung Ones*
4. *Gnomes Under the Hammer*
5. *Pooh Wants to Be a Millionaire?*

Romcom Movies

1. *Jeepless in Seattle*
2. *My Big Fat Greek Shredding*
3. *Bridget Jones's Priory*
4. *Rotting Hill*
5. *You've Got Quail*

GAME 34: WATCH YOUR BREATH

1. Kiefer-Sutherland-*Keeping-Up-Appearances*-Scarlett-Johansson-*(What's-the-Story)-Morning-Glory?*

2. Arnold-Schwarzenegger-Wolverhampton-Wanderers-*On-Her-Majesty's-Secret-Service-One-Foot-in-the-Grave*

3. Louisa-May-Alcott-*How-to-Lose-a-Guy-in-10-Days-Fantastic-Beasts-and-Where-to-Find-Them*-Helena-Bonham-Carter

4. *Lock,-Stock-and-Two-Smoking-Barrels*-F.-Scott-Fitzgerald-'Itsy-Bitsy-Teeny-Weeny-Yellow-Polka-Dot-Bikini'-Sports-Personality-of-the-Year

GAME 35: SEE MY GUESTS

GUEST ONE

For 8 points: Non-renewable

For 6 points: Royal blue

For 4 points: Blue-collar

For 2 points: Anne Boleyn

Answer: Laurence Llewelyn-Bowen

GUEST TWO

For 8 points: Hillary

For 6 points: Éclair

For 4 points: Harley

For 2 points: 'Reach'

Answer: Rachel Riley

SET 9 SCORECARD

	Player 1	Player 2	Player 3	Player 4
Game 33				
Game 34				
Game 35				
Game 36				
Totals				

WINNER!

SET 10

... in which you must stifle a tune

GAME 37
CROSSED WIRES

You need: some noise-makers: bells, drums, or simply spatulas and a tin

Players: 4 or more, but an even number

Scoring: see below

Welcome to the Arbitration Room. It's hardly divulging a trade secret if we tell you that some of the *House of Games* pairs games are designed so that a cowardly contestant who doesn't buzz in feels mildly awkward in themselves and, at the same time, a guest who does buzz in risks causing awkwardness for their partner and the other players as well as themselves.

The Arbitration Room is where, after testing out such games and repeatedly landing each other in it, we hug it out ...

– I do apologise: I was *certain* the title was 'Don't You Want Me Baby'.

– And I apologise too: I thought you'd *remember* it was just 'Don't You Want Me' because I'd rejected *your* question about the song for the Elephant in the Room 'Baby' category, and you're not normally *quite* so forgetful.

... that sort of thing.

Case in point: Crossed Wires. **Get in pairs and sit back to back so you can't communicate. When you buzz in, it's your partner who will answer**, beginning their response 'I am ...'. If they're right, you both get 1 point; otherwise, everyone else gets 1 point.

1. I used the name Polly Baker

    I swam with wooden 'fins' attached to my hands

    I am credited with coining the phrase 'nothing is certain but death and taxes'

    While an ambassador in France, I became an unlikely fashion icon

    I invented bifocal lenses, the lightning rod and the glass harmonica

    I appear on the $100 bill and my name is often used as slang for it

    I was a founding father of the United States

2. I married a newsreader in 2006

    My uncle is the Earl of Huntingdon

    I was schoolfriends with Miranda Hart

    I've written an autobiography called *My Animals and Other Family*

    I've presented Olympic coverage, horse-racing, Wimbledon and Crufts

3.   I have a national holiday in May in my home country

I was played by Ingrid Bergman in a 1948 film

I was a key figure during the Hundred Years War

I believed that I was able to speak directly to God

I was born in the village of Domrémy in the early 1400s

I am the patron saint of France

4 .   In 1981, I went to a South Shields nightclub

I switched on the Blackpool Lights

I was the son of Mared and Quorum

There is a statue of me in Southport, Merseyside

After I retired I was ridden by Lee Mack

I have won the Grand National more times than any other horse

My name is chanted in *The Shining*

I have been a guest at the Sports Personality of the Year awards

ANSWERS
See page 164

GAME 38
HOUSE OF GAMERS

You need: nothing extra

Players: any number

Scoring: 2 points per correct answer

We've added a letter to the title of some books and songs. We'll give you a synopsis of the new title, and you tell us what that title is.

For example, if the clue for a Bond film was 'Pierce Brosnan puts off eating more salad', you would answer not 'Die Another Day' but ... that's right: 'Diet Another Day'.

FOUR-LETTER COUNTRIES

(yielding five-letter answers)

1. A landlocked West African country which spent its teenage years in the White House.

2. An island which can breathe underwater while diving around the Caribbean.

3. A neighbour of Vietnam which doubles up as Africa's second-biggest city.

4. A landlocked Central African country which is increasingly popular as a salad 'superfood'.

5. An Arabian sultanate which hosts a good-natured BBC tea-time quiz.

CAROLS AND HYMNS

1. Heavenly creatures wish 'glory to' the newborn deadly fish.

2. The Lord God made each and every animal in an American shopping complex.

3. With the words 'Let nothing you dismay', festive cheer comes when some chaps are turned off and on again.

4. This carol considers whether *Robinson Crusoe* or *Daniel Defoe* has the better claim to be the earliest example of a literary genre.

5. A favourite of the terraces, this hymn describes a desire to move in with the star of *Sleepless in Seattle*.

ANSWERS
See page 164

GAME 39
BROKEN KARAOKE

You need: nothing

Players: 2 or more (plus 1 to read out the questions)

Scoring: 2 points for every correct answer

If you're reading the questions, first give the year. Then **read out the initials to the lyrics from a well-known passage in a well-known pop song.** Try to match them to the song – for example, if the song contains a very long 'yeeeeeeeeeaaaaaaaaaaaaaah', say a curt, simple 'Y', then wait until giving the next letter.

TRY TO STAY ON ONE NOTE. This is not a game about melody. It's pure words, all the way.

If you don't know a song, skip it (or just give it your best shot on the basis that it's not your problem).

And if they don't get it the first time, just read it again, and again …

1. *Year: 1973*   YUTSLALL
                      (YKYDYKYDYKYD)
                      BITECWIWWL
                      MYGIAC
                      SLALD
                      (LALD)
                      LALD
                      (LALD)

2. *Year: 1994*   IDNTHMS
                      TUTF
                      SCWMMH
                      WATOCD
                      IJWYFMO
                      MTYCEK
                      MMWCT
                      AIWFCIY

3. *Year: 1961*   I T J
    (and others)   T M J

                           T L S T

                           I T J

                           T Q J

                           T L S T H H

                           W D H W A A

                           (A W W A W W A W W A W W)

                           (A W W A W W A W W A W W)

4. *Year: 1970*   L A B O T W

                           I W L M D

                           L A B O T W

                           I W L M D

5. *Year: 1984*   W M U B Y G-G

                           D L M H O L A Y

                           W M U B Y G-G

                           I D W T M I W Y H T H

ANSWERS

See page 164

GAME 40

STICK IT: PEOPLE FROM BOOKS

You need: pencils and a phone with a clock app

Players: 2 or more

Scoring: 2 points if someone guesses your drawing;
2 points if you guess someone else's drawing

When you've been watching the guests play Stick It on the telly, you've certainly been saying to yourself: 'I wish I could play this game with friends and family. I've got the pencils, I've got the willingness, but I just don't have access to the templates that make the game so irresistible.'

We hear you. And so, after a lengthy and baffling tussle with Corporate Affairs, we are pretty sure we can share with you the House of Games Stick Person.

Go to the answers at the end of this set, block off the whole page, then move down to the last section, headed STICK IT. The first player should then look at the first answer only, the second should look at the second answer only, and so on.

They then have 20 seconds to draw on one of the Stick People below, during which everyone else will shout out who on earth they think is being depicted. Wrong answers are *not* frozen out. Good luck!

ANSWERS
See page 164

158

1.

2.

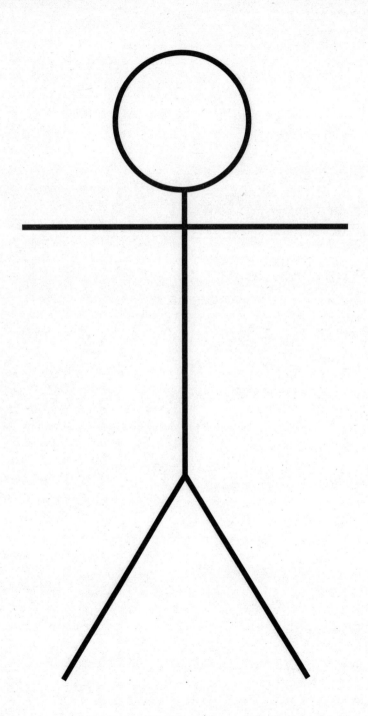

3.

4.

5.

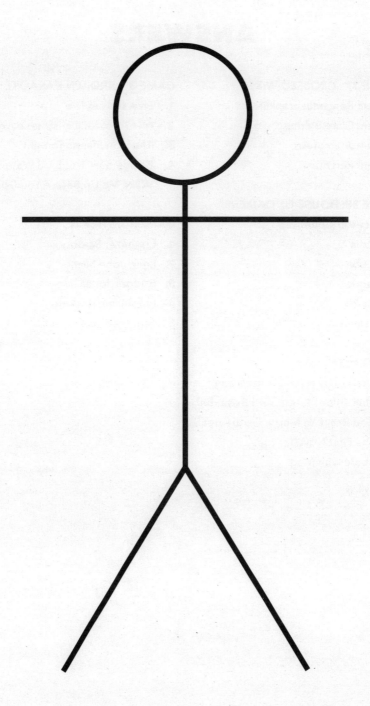

ANSWERS

GAME 37 : CROSSED WIRES

1. I am Benjamin Franklin
2. I am Clare Balding
3. I am Joan of Arc
4. I am Red Rum

GAME 38: HOUSE OF GAMERS

Four-Letter Countries

1. Malia
2. Scuba
3. Lagos
4. Chard
5. Osman

Carols and Hymns

1. 'Shark! The Herald Angels Sing'
2. 'Mall Things Bright And Beautiful'
3. 'God Reset Ye Merry, Gentlemen'
4. 'The First Novel'
5. 'Abide with Meg'

GAME 39: BROKEN KARAOKE

1. 'Live and Let Die'
2. 'All I Want for Christmas is You'
3. 'The Lion Sleeps Tonight'
4. 'Bridge over Troubled Water'
5. 'Wake Me Up Before You Go-Go'

GAME 40: STICK IT

1. Ebenezer Scrooge
2. Long John Silver
3. Bridget Jones
4. Pippi Longstocking
5. Jemima Puddle-Duck

SET 10 SCORECARD			
	Player 1	Player 2	Player 3	Player 4
Game 37				
Game 38				
Game 39				
Game 40				
Totals				

WINNER!

SET 11

... in which you will name a monster

GAME 41
HORSE OF JAMES

You need: nothing more

Players: any number

Scoring: 5 points for the first to shout each category

Fun Fact: Question Writers Day Off was conceived for the first *House of Games* book before it became a staple of the TV show. Apropos of nothing, here's a little wordplay game we've been trying out.

In this game, you get points if you're first to identify the category. **We'll show you three things in that category, with a single letter having changed in the more important words.**

Cover the text below, and reveal the info gradually. Ignore punctuation.

CATEGORY ONE

Break Horse

Ward Nîmes

A Sale of Tao Cuties

CATEGORY TWO

Gran

He-Men

Omen

CATEGORY THREE

Reads Steamy Book

Wary Beery Cocks

The Faked Cher

CATEGORY FOUR

Tie

Noon

Iran

ANSWERS
See page 176

GAME 42
WHERE IS KAZAKHSTAN?

You need: a phone or tablet each

Players: 2 or more

Scoring: 4 points for each correct answer

When you watch *House of Games* guests playing this geography game, do you ever kid yourself that you would commit less shameful errors if you got the chance to play? Kid yourself no more.*

Open a map app on your device, and pinch it until the named continent fills the screen.

Tap and hold where *you think* the named landmark is. Be careful, you only get one go at this.

Now ask for directions (on foot), and enter the name of the landmark as your destination. Compare your results: whoever is closest gets the 2 points each time. Remember to cancel everything before your next 'journey'.**

---

* Although we're certain you know which way up Africa goes (series 4, week 7).

** They're only pretend journeys, of course; if you want a real one, we can thoroughly recommend heading to Norfolk's Horsey Windpump and were delighted to give Jo Caulfield the opportunity to share this windmill with a wider audience in 2022.

1. *Continent:* Europe

   Destination: The Tivoli Gardens

2. *Continent:* Asia

   Destination: The Tokyo Stock Exchange

3. *Continent:* Africa

   Destination: Fez

4. *Continent:* North America

   Destination: The Lincoln Memorial

5. *Continent:* Europe

   Destination: The headquarters of Dundee City Council

GAME 43
AND THE ANSWER ISN'T

Take it in turns to be the guesser. **You're asked a question. Everyone else writes down a plausible answer, and someone also writes the real answer,** then reads all the answers in random order.

Win 3 points if you can identify the real answer; otherwise the points go to the player who fooled you.

1. The UK street with the longest name is found in the New Forest. What's it called?

2. What is the real name of the Muppet nicknamed 'Cookie Monster'?

3. In 2017, why did Genoa Airport relax its 'no liquids' security rule?

4. What remarkable feat was achieved by Albert II on 14 June 1949?

5. When he was a guest on *Desert Island Discs* in 2006, what did Simon Cowell predictably choose as his luxury item?

6. What does the first 'D' stand for in 'D-Day'?

ANSWERS

See page 176

GAME 44
ROONERSPISMS

You need: noise-makers to work as buzzers

Players: any number

Scoring: 2 per complete pair of answers

Welcome to the Room of Regrets. This is where we work on certain games, including the one based on spoonerisms, the form of wordplay where you swap the sounds at the beginnings of words.

Usually, we name our games in a way that immediately tells guests, viewers and readers what they're expected to do. 'Mouse Of Games': change a letter. 'Only Fools And Zebras': swap a word for something similar. The reasons this game is compiled in the Room of Regrets are: (a) its name only makes sense if you already understand the concept and (b) we somehow did not name it 'Gouse of Hames'. But perhaps it was always on borrowed time?

Give the two answers each time, remembering that they are spoonerisms of each other. For example, if the clues were 'Head louse' and 'Tight embrace', you would say: 'Hair bug and bear hug'. Bingers on fuzzers.

1. Reply to 'Where's the Colosseum, darlin'?'

   Baseball hit that leaves the playing area

2. Ensnare pointy-eared *Star Trek* character

   Cut, flatten and grill a chicken

3. Dismiss a couple of batsmen

   Creature that *His Dark Materials'* Iorek Byrnison resembles

4. A conger that protects a castle

   Ingredient of flapjacks and porridge

5. Put a sirloin on the scales

   Anti-lullaby in *Mary Poppins*

6. An introduction, to Mr Starmer, of Mr Hancock

   Creature represented by Aleksandr Orlov, the price-comparison mascot

7. What a frequently escaped prison needs

   Mel Giedroyc's Hangman-esque BBC quiz

8. Cycle past London's Somerset House

   Maestro's instruction to get the musicians started

ANSWERS
See page 176

ANSWERS

GAME 41 : HORSE OF JAMES

CATEGORY ONE: Dickens novels

CATEGORY TWO: Middle Eastern countries

CATEGORY THREE: TV cookery shows

CATEGORY FOUR: Chemical elements

GAME 43: AND THE ANSWER ISN'T

1. Bolderwood Arboretum Ornamental Drive

2. Sidney Monster

3. So passengers can carry enormous jars of pesto

4. He became the first monkey in space

5. A mirror

6. Day

GAME 44: ROONERSPISMS

1. 'Rome, hun' / Home run

2. Catch Spock / Spatchcock

3. Bowl a pair / Polar bear

4. Moat eel / Oatmeal

5. Weigh a steak / 'Stay Awake'

6. 'Keir, Matt' / Meerkat

7. Better locks / *Letterbox*

8. Bike up the Strand / Strike up the band

SET 11 SCORECARD			
	Player 1	Player 2	Player 3	Player 4
Game 41				
Game 42				
Game 43				
Game 44				
Totals				

WINNER!

SET 12

... in which a coconut may be a horse
but it may not be a coconut

GAME 45
HAIKU YOU

You need: a poetical disposition

Players: any number

Scoring: 5 points per moment identified

We like haiku at House of Games. Rigid, unwavering structure, terse form, mathematical symmetry: what's not to savour? Just two problems: (1) haiku don't have answers; (2) their purpose is to evoke a Zen-like appreciation of a moment in nature.

The second thing is especially baffling, really: we don't tend to leave the House of Games, so moments in nature really aren't a 'thing' for us. We're happy to announce that we've improved this centuries-old format and repurposed it for quiz.

Each of these haiku describes a memorable moment ... from *telly.* Get someone to read them out ponderously; yell when enlightenment dawns.

1.   One minute to go

     Wolstenholme yells in delight

     They haven't won since

2.   A fireplace behind

     'So it was a bit crowded'

     The Queen doesn't know

3.   Panthers, Patriots

     Then for half of a second

     A body part's seen

4.   He's tall and she's not

     Bros fans drown everything out

     Wrong winners announced

ANSWERS
See page 190

GAME 46
THE Z LIST

Again, **you get 1 point if your answer fits the category, 3 points if yours is the last alphabetically of everyone playing and 5 points if yours is the answer that comes last alphabetically of all the acceptable answers that we kindly provide.** Cover up the possible answers.

Ignore, please, any 'The's or 'A's etc. at the beginning of possible answers. That's standard.

SQUARES ON A MONOPOLY BOARD
(London, of course)

The Angel, Islington	Marlborough Street
Bond Street	Marylebone Station
Bow Street	Mayfair
Chance	Northumberland Avenue
Community Chest	Old Kent Road
Coventry Street	Oxford Street
Electric Company	Pall Mall
Euston Road	Park Lane
Fenchurch Street Station	Pentonville Road
Fleet Street	Piccadilly
Free Parking	Regent Street
Go	Strand
Go To Jail	Super Tax
In Jail	Trafalgar Square
Income Tax	Vine Street
Just Visiting	Water Works
King's Cross Station	Whitechapel Road
Leicester Square	Whitehall
Liverpool Street Station	

ASIAN CAPITAL CITIES
(we're doing the 'wholly-or-partly-in-Asia' thing)

Abu Dhabi	Dushanbe	Phnom Penh
Amman	Hanoi	Pyongyang
Ankara	Islamabad	Riyadh
Ashgabat	Jakarta	Sanaa
Baghdad	Jerusalem	Seoul
Baku	Kabul	Singapore
Bandar Seri Begawan	Kathmandu	Taipei
Bangkok	Kuala Lumpur	Tashkent
Beijing	Kuwait City	Tbilisi
Beirut	Male	Tehran
Bishkek	Manama	Thimphu
Colombo	Manila	Tokyo
Damascus	Moscow	Ulaanbaatar
Delhi	Muscat	Vientiane
Dhaka	Nay Pyi Taw	Yerevan
Dili	Nicosia	
Doha	Nursultan	

SONGS FROM THE ORIGINAL LONDON CAST RECORDING OF OLIVER!

(that's 1960 – no reprises or finales, please)

'As Long As He Needs Me'

'Be Back Soon'

'Boy for Sale'

'Consider Yourself'

'Food, Glorious Food'

'I Shall Scream'

'I'd Do Anything'

'It's a Fine Life'

'My Name'

'Oliver'

'Oom-Pah-Pah'

'Reviewing the Situation'

'That's Your Funeral'

'Where Is Love?'

'Who Will Buy?'

'You've Got to Pick a Pocket or Two'

PARTIES WHICH WON A SEAT IN THE 2019 GENERAL ELECTION
(spelled out in full – and yes, that is a hint)

Alliance Party of Northern Ireland

Conservative Party

Democratic Unionist Party

Green Party of England and Wales

Labour Party

Liberal Democrats

Plaid Cymru

Scottish National Party

Sinn Féin

Social Democratic and Labour Party

GAME 47
TOTES EMOJI

We are now in The Den, where we enjoy a spot of TV. Sadly, we are the only people in the UK who can't properly enjoy watching *House of Games** because we know the answers. Most of them, that is. Totes Emoji is a favourite of ours because even the question setter who's come up with the titles has no idea what the guests might put, or how much detail they might use. Compare, for example, Gareth Malone's entire plot …

… of *The Gruffalo* to David O'Doherty's, shall we say 'sideways' take …

… on *The Vicar of Dibley.***

---

*   Aside from the odd relative who watches occasionally and says something like 'What strange minds you must all have' without realising how obvious it is that they disliked the programme.

** The tricolour is, it seems, a clue to the lead actor's name.

Cover up the titles below. **Take it in turns to compose a text message which conveys the answer using only emojis.** Send to everyone else in the room and see who gets the answer first. You get 1 point and so do they.

FILM MUSICALS

1. *Mamma Mia!*

2. *Fame*

3. *Little Shop of Horrors*

4. *La La Land*

5. *The Greatest Showman*

CHILDREN'S BOOKS

1. *Danny the Champion of the World*

2. *Little Miss Bossy*

3. *The Voyage of the Dawn Treader*

4. *Asterix the Gaul*

5. *Where's Spot?*

GAME 48
SOUNDING OFF

You need: see below

Players: 2 or more

Scoring: see below

You can use anything except: language and any kind of drawing.

Cover the list below and take it in turns to reveal a moment in history. **You must then convey that moment using sound alone.** You can scour the surrounding area for anything to make noises, but they must also be *aural* clues: coconuts would be OK for Lady Godiva's tour of Coventry (as in, coconuts can represent the sound of a horse's hooves), but not for, say, the discovery of the Solomon Islands (as in, coconuts cannot represent coconuts).

Each time someone gets an answer right, they get 2 points, and so does the person making the (non-verbal) sounds. Multiple guesses are more than welcome.

1.   The Berlin Wall falls

2.   Edmund Hillary and Tenzing Norgay reach the summit of Everest

3.   Alexander Fleming discovers penicillin

4.   Julius Caesar is assassinated

5.   The dodo becomes extinct

ANSWERS

GAME 45: HAIKU YOU

1. The 1966 World Cup final
2. Martin Bashir's Diana interview
3. Super Bowl XXXVIII
4. The 1989 Brit Awards

SET 12 SCORECARD			
	Player 1	Player 2	Player 3	Player 4
Game 45				
Game 46				
Game 47				
Game 48				
Totals				

WINNER!

SET 13

... in which you may choose
not to eat humble pie

GAME 49
HOSE OF GAMES

You need: nothing

Players: any number, take it in turns

Scoring: 2 points for every correct answer

We're back in the Mouse Annexe!

An opposing player will read you a description of a TV show, poem, etc. **It is entirely made-up, but it is also a real TV show, poem, etc. with one letter removed.**

So if the description of a TV show was 'In New York City, we follow the romantic adventures of six demonic twentysomethings', you would reply not *Friends* but *Fiends*.

COMEDY FILMS

1. Vince Vaughn and Owen Wilson invade various nuptials in order to steal bacon.

2. Los Angeles teen Cher Horowitz matchmakes her friends but is ill-equipped when it comes to playing snooker.

3. In ancient Egypt, a beautiful queen falls in love with the male lead in *Titanic* (played by Sid James).

4. Marilyn Monroe and Jane Russell visit their GPs, who chivalrously send both of them off to see specialists.

5. Matthew Broderick calls Jim Carrey to fix his TV and finds that he's remarkably competent.

CHILDREN'S BOOKS

1. Roald Dahl tells the tale of three farmers, constantly outsmarted by a castrated bull.

2. In this epic adventure tale, a group of rabbits searching for a new warren try their luck on the New York stock market.

3. By finding a golden ticket, a boy is granted entry to Simon Cowell's magical confectionery-based talent show.

4. After years of playing the Hulk, actor Mark hides in the woods, where he meets a mouse taking a stroll ...

5. In an old chalk pit, Barney finds a caveman who is active in the Northern Ireland political scene.

ANSWERS
See page 202

GAME 50
DON'T MENTION IT!

You need: phone with countdown on the clock app

Players: 2 or more

Scoring: 3 points every time you manage to answer correctly

This is one of our games where we take a straightforward challenge and ~~make it disagreeable~~ add a *House of Games* twist.

Take it in turns to read out the following categories to one other player. **They have three seconds to name anything in that category … apart from the forbidden answers** that you'll also read out before pressing START on the clock app. Feel free to loudly bark 'Start!' for extra edginess.

BOROUGHS OF NEW YORK

Except for: Manhattan, Brooklyn, The Bronx

PERMANENT MEMBERS OF THE
UN SECURITY COUNCIL

Except for: USA, Russia, China

TWENTY-FIRST-CENTURY TV SERIES CREATED BY RUSSELL T DAVIES

Except for: Queer as Folk, Doctor Who, It's a Sin

EUROPEAN FIZZY WINES

Except for: Cava, Prosecco, Champagne

PIERCE BROSNAN BOND FILMS

Except for: Tomorrow Never Dies, Die Another Day, GoldenEye

NAMES IN LOU BEGA'S SONG 'MAMBO NO. 5'

Except for: Tina, Erica, Monica

ANSWERS
See page 202

GAME 51
OFFAL OR WAFFLE

You need: pencil and paper
Players: any number
Scoring: 2 points per correct allocation

Take your pencil and paper, and for each of the dishes below **mark whether you think it is a genuine dish made from some creature or creatures' internal parts ('offal') or one that we've imagined ('waffle').**

If at the end of the game any players have decided to go vegan, do let us know as we will be eligible for some kind of grant, plus we can carbon-offset it against the vintage Japanese pinball machines Richard keeps ordering online.

Head Cheese	Drib
Love in Disguise	Everything-Else Cake
Loggins' Scrapings	Pet Stick
Lancashire Lobes	Humble Pie
Splumb	Dark Biscuits

ANSWERS
See page 202

GAME 52
E, I, E, I ... OH!

You need: nothing

Players: any number

Scoring: 3 points per correct category

Block off the text below. Slowly reveal the items, one at a time. These are four items from a category with their vowels altered.

As soon as you think you know the category to which the items belong, give your guess. Then privately look at the answers on page 202: if you're right, take the 3 points; if not, re-cover the clues as they were and step out with good grace.

CATEGORY ONE

NANO

FEAR

SAX

OUGHT

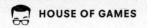
CATEGORY TWO

FAMER

POTILLO

TEBEO

FEBALO

CATEGORY THREE

LALA

ODALA

TAM JANIS

SHORLAY BISSAY

CATEGORY FOUR

GIGGLA

PORLEOMINT

MERDOR

SWIRM

CATEGORY FIVE

OROBISQAI

GLOSSIDU

PARIEOTTO

PUS DA CHUT

CATEGORY SIX

ROTUBUGU

IRAGALI

ZECCHANA

IGGPLUNT

CATEGORY SEVEN

SMELL

JOLLY

SNOOZO

STRING

ANSWERS
See page 202

See page 202

ANSWERS

GAME 49: HOSE OF GAMES

Comedy Films

1. *Wedding Rashers*
2. *Cueless*
3. *Carry On Leo*
4. *Gentlemen Refer Blondes*
5. *The Able Guy*

Children's Books

1. *Fantastic Mr Ox*
2. *Watership Dow*
3. *Charlie and the Chocolate Factor*
4. *The Ruffalo*
5. *Stig of the DUP*

GAME 50: DON'T MENTION IT!

BOROUGHS OF NEW YORK:
   Queen's/Staten Island

PERMANENT MEMBERS OF THE UN
   SECURITY COUNCIL: France/UK

TWENTY-FIRST-CENTURY TV SERIES
   CREATED BY RUSSELL T. DAVIES:
   *Banana/Bob & Rose/Casanova/
   Cucumber/Mine All Mine/The
   Sarah Jane Adventures/The Second
   Coming/Tofu/Torchwood/Years
   and Years*

EUROPEAN FIZZY WINES: Asti/
   Crémant/Franciacorta/Lambrusco/
   Sekt/some fancy fizz you've heard
   of and we have yet to encounter

PIERCE BROSNAN BOND FILMS:
   The World Is Not Enough

NAMES IN LOU BEGA'S SONG
   'MAMBO No. 5': Angela/Jessica/
   Mary/Pamela/Rita/Sandra

GAME 51: OFFAL OR WAFFLE

The genuine ones are:

Head Cheese (a jellied loaf made from
   a pig's head, AKA brawn)

Love in Disguise (calf's heart wrapped
   in minced veal and coated with
   vermicelli)

Drob (lamb membrane stuffed with
   lamb intestines and milk)

Pet Stick (traditional butcher's treat for
   his or her own dog)

Humble Pie (originally meaning a pie
   of a deer's heart and entrails)

GAME 52: E, I, E, I … OH!

CATEGORY ONE: Basic numbers

CATEGORY TWO: Bones in your leg

CATEGORY THREE: James Bond
   theme vocalists

CATEGORY FOUR: Groups of animals

CATEGORY FIVE: Ballet terminology

CATEGORY SIX: Names Americans
   mistakenly use for vegetables

CATEGORY SEVEN: Mr Men

SET 13 SCORECARD			
	Player 1	Player 2	Player 3	Player 4
Game 49				
Game 50				
Game 51				
Game 52				
Totals				

WINNER!

SET 14

... in which one of you will
be a Richard

GAME 53
SEE MY GUESTS

You need: to block off parts of the following pages as you go

Players: any number (and someone to check your guesses)

Scoring: see below

You'll see two images of guests from the TV version of *House of Games*. If you can tell who they are straightaway, that's *10 points each*. (Get someone else to check, in case you're wrong.)

If you can't, then there are some questions underneath, of the kind we use in our round It's All In The Name. As that name suggests, this will give you some of the letters of the guest's name. But each time you use one of these questions, *the points available go down by 2*.

Cooperation and inspiration: and you'll all boost your scores.

GUEST ONE

For 10 points:

Can you name them?

Answer these questions to get some of the letters in their name.

For 8 points:

Delicious item also known as 'tomato fruit'

For 6 points:

Occupation of Anna Pavlova and Margot Fonteyn

For 4 points:

Elvis's opulent Memphis homestead

For 2 points:

Haircare device named after a Lewis Carroll character

GUEST TWO

For 10 points:

Can you name them?

Answer these questions to get some of the letters in their name.

For 8 points:

More usual name for plebiscites

For 6 points:

Places for pots or places for tots

For 4 points:

Places for sisters, religiously speaking

For 2 points:

Disciples of Sigmund

ANSWERS
See page 220

GAME 54
DON'T STATE THE OBVIOUS

Pair 1 should look at the first answer on page 220 and whisper it to one player in Pair 2.

Pair 1 then write down three words that they think the player in Pair 2 will use to describe the answer to their partner. The player in Pair 2 then says their three chosen words. If their partner guesses correctly, both players in Pair 2 get 1 point - unless Pair 1 has guessed any of the words used, in which case no-one gets anything.

ANSWERS
See page 220

GAME 55

STICK IT: PEOPLE FROM HISTORY

You need: pencils and a phone with a clock app

Players: 2 or more

Scoring: 2 points if someone guesses your drawing;
2 points if you guess someone else's drawing

Go to the answers at the end of this set, **block off the whole page,** then move down to the last section, headed STICK IT. The first player should then look at the first answer only, the second should look at the second answer only, and so on.

They then have 20 seconds to draw on one of the Stick People below, during which everyone else will shout out who on earth they think is being depicted. Wrong answers are *not* frozen out. Good luck!

ANSWERS
See page 220

1.

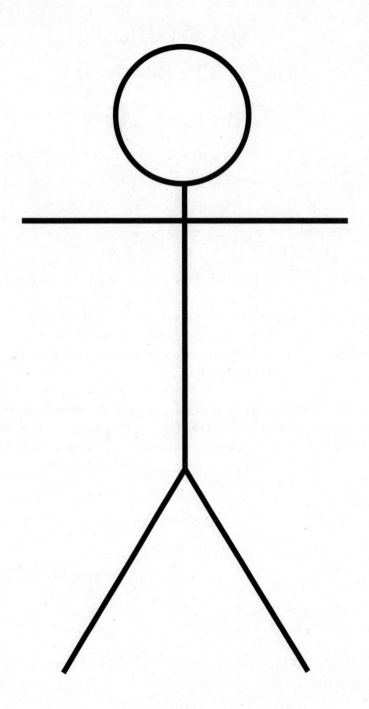

2.

3.

4.

5.

GAME 56
THE RICH LIST

For this game you need a Richard. We're lucky at the House of Games in that we always have our own Richard, plus of course a team of Standby Richards: Wilson, Ayoade, E. Grant and, if needs absolutely must, Herring.

So who will your Richard be?

If one of you is named Richard, they will be your Richard. If two of you are named Richard: (a) congratulations and (b) your Richard must be whichever of the Richards' surname is alphabetically closer to 'Osman'.

If you have no Richards, you may have a temporary Honorary Richard. This should be whichever of you most resembles our own Richard: in temperament, not appearance.

Once you're ready, block off the next page and reveal only the first category. **All players write down something in that category. You get 5 points only if your answer is correct *and* you're the only person who chose it.**

But if anyone's answer is the same as your Richard's, all points in that category are annulled. Sorry.

ANY COUNTY OF THE UK ...

... located in Wales (and that's modern ceremonial counties/principal areas, for those who enjoy such distinctions)

Anglesey	Merthyr Tydfil
Blaenau Gwent	Monmouthshire
Bridgend	Neath Port Talbot
Caerphilly	Newport
Cardiff	Pembrokeshire
Carmarthenshire	Powys
Ceredigion	Rhondda Cynon Taff
Conwy	Swansea
Denbighshire	Torfaen
Flintshire	Vale of Glamorgan
Gwynedd	Wrexham

ANY INGREDIENT IN BBC GOOD FOOD'S SEAFOOD PAELLA RECIPE ...

... that's suitable for fish-avoiding vegetarians

Broad beans	Olive oil	Parsley
Cayenne pepper	Onion	Peas
Chopped tomatoes	Paella rice	Saffron
Garlic	Paprika	Star anise

ANY CHRONICLES OF NARNIA BOOK ...

... with no animal in the title

Prince Caspian

The Voyage of the Dawn Treader

The Silver Chair

The Magician's Nephew

The Last Battle

ANY WEDDING ANNIVERSARY GIFT ...

... apart from metals, gems or precious stones

China	Ivory	Silk
Cotton	Lace	Sugar
Crystal	Leather	Wood
Electrical appliance	Linen	Wool
Flowers	Paper	
Fruit	Pottery	

ANSWERS

GAME 53: SEE MY GUESTS

For 8 points: Grenadilla

For 6 points: Ballerina

For 4 points: Graceland

For 2 points: Alice band

Answer: Clare Balding

GUEST TWO

For 8 points: Referenda

For 6 points: Nurseries

For 4 points: Nunneries

For 2 points: Freudians

Answer: Jennifer Saunders

GAME 54: DON'T STATE THE OBVIOUS

Elizabeth I

Gondola

Scrabble

The Channel Tunnel

Crufts

Apple pie

Eton mess

Mardi Gras

Angel of the North

Polo

GAME 55: STICK IT

1. Isambard Kingdom Brunel
2. Margaret Thatcher
3. Sigmund Freud
4. Anne Boleyn
5. Emmeline Pankhurst

SET 14 SCORECARD			
	Player 1	Player 2	Player 3	Player 4
Game 53				
Game 54				
Game 55				
Game 56				
Totals				

WINNER!

SET 15

... in which one of you will
pretend to be Keith Richards

GAME 57
BID UP YOURSELF

Nominate one player as the Auctioneer, who will read each question aloud.

Other players then shout their guesses. You have a maximum of three per player, and each guess must be more than the previous.

When no-one wishes to take any more guesses, the highest guesser gets 4 points. But if the Auctioneer announces that a guess has gone *over* the actual answer, points are annulled for that question. Sorry. I'd say that we don't make the rules but that's literally one of the most important things we do.

1. How many years did the Hundred Years War actually last?

2. At the time of writing, how many homes does Jeff Bezos have?

3. How many EU member states use the euro?

4. On the covers of the books, how many Mr. Men are wearing a hat?

5. How many times is a swear word spoken in the film *The Wolf of Wall Street?*

ANSWERS
See page 232

GAME 58
I PUT A SPELL ON YOU

One of the most important aspects of a game is its name. We have a firm policy at House of Games of choosing the best name possible for each game and, even if we later think of something else, sticking to our choice. Except for games like this one, which is currently called You Spell Terrible.

You play in pairs. Choose wisely.

Buzz in when you think you know the answer. Then your partner must try to spell the answer. If both answer and spelling are correct, you get 1 point each.

If you're the one reading the questions, get them to do the spelling slowly and make some sort of positive or negative sound after each letter to really ramp up the tension.

1. What's the day before Good Friday?

2. Who created the Mr. Men series?*

3. What's the golfing term for one stroke over par?

4. Because applause is forbidden in the House of Commons, what do MPs call out instead?

5. What's the name of the fancy art exhibition held in Venice every two years?

6. Set on a Scottish island, which children's TV series featured the characters PC Plum and Miss Hoolie?

7. What's twenty-two times two?

8. Harry Houdini set a record for escaping from what restrictive item of clothing?

9. Which Spanish soprano duetted with Freddie Mercury on the Olympic theme song 'Barcelona'?

10. What term means 'to specify incorrectly the letters in a word'?

ANSWERS
See page 232

---

*   I find the Mr. Men so useful in quiz that Howard, who copy-edited this book, has begun to address me as 'Mr. "The Mr. Men" Man'; another literary reference we return to time and again on the show is a certain novel of 1844. I won't name it, but once you notice it...

GAME 59
THE NICE ROUND: ANIMALS

You need: pencil and paper

Players: ideally 4

Scoring: see below

Cover the list at the end of this set so that only the first animal is visible.

Now, take it in turns to be the guesser. **Each time, everyone who isn't the guesser reads the answer and writes down a one-word clue to help the guesser.**

After the guesser has been shown all three clues, they give their guess. They get 1 point if they're right, and also award 1 point to whichever player they think has been most helpful.*

ANSWERS
See page 232

---

* Keener viewers may remember the time we tried The Not-So-Nice Round, where points were to be deducted for the least helpful clue. Our guests were literally so nice that they broke the format. Which isn't at all to say, dear reader, that it might not work in your group.

GAME 60
RHYME TIME

You need: no extra materials; just this book

Players: someone to read, and ideally 2 or more players

Scoring: 2 points for every correct answer

You know Rhyme Time. **You get a pair of clues. There's a pair of answers. And the answers rhyme.**

If you're reading the clues, choose someone and read them the first pair: 2 points if they get both right; if not, pass it to the right until someone does, for 1 point.

Either way, play *then* passes to the right.

1.   **More normal way of saying 'fourscore'**

     Wyclef Jean's Caribbean country of birth

2.   **Primate with hairless buttocks**

     Largest woodwind

3. Type of antelope that teaches Peppa Pig's class

    Singer with albums *19*, *21*, *25* and *30*

4. Martial art with name meaning 'empty hand'

    High-register male singers of the seventeenth and eighteenth centuries

5. Paul Young's banging duet with Zucchero

    'Nothing Compares 2 U' hitmaker

6. Naughty dog who chased deer in Richmond Park in 2011

    Keeley Hawes's troubled *Line of Duty* character

7. Male competitor in the America's Cup race

    Sister newspaper to *Scotland on Sunday*

8. Thick white sauce flavoured with onion

    Composer known almost solely for his Canon in D

9. First female US vice president

    French-set Lily Collins romcom series

10. What 'PCR' stands for in 'PCR test'

    Rolling Stones song with this guitar riff*

ANSWERS

See page 232

---

* If you're the one reading this out, do the riff with your voice: DUNH DUNH duh-duh-
DUNH duh duh-duh duh-duh.

ANSWERS

GAME 57: BID UP YOURSELF

1. 116
2. 10
3. 19
4. 33
5. 715

GAME 58: I PUT A SPELL ON YOU

1. Maundy Thursday
2. Roger Hargreaves
3. Bogey
4. 'Hear, hear'
5. Biennale
6. *Balamory*
7. Forty-four
8. Straitjacket (your choice whether or not to also accept 'straightjacket')
9. Montserrat Caballé (your choice whether or not to be lenient about the accent)
10. Misspell

GAME 59: THE NICE ROUND

Chipmunk
Labradoodle
Dragonfly
Chameleon
Shetland pony
Penguin
Pot-bellied pig

GAME 60: RHYME TIME

1. Eighty
   Haiti
2. Baboon
   Bassoon
3. Gazelle
   Adele
4. Karate
   Castrati
5. 'Senza una donna'
   Sinéad O'Connor
6. Fenton
   Lindsay Denton
7. Yachtsman
   The *Scotsman*
8. Béchamel
   Pachelbel
9. Kamala Harris
   Emily in Paris
10. Polymerase chain reaction
    '(I Can't Get No) Satisfaction'

SET 15 SCORECARD			
	Player 1	Player 2	Player 3	Player 4
Game 57				
Game 58				
Game 59				
Game 60				
Totals				

WINNER!

SET 16

... in which you'll imagine
being chased by a dinosaur

GAME 61
GAMES HOUSE OF ...

You need: more nothing

Players: any number plus questions read someone the to

Scoring: answer correct each for points 2

Alphabetical answers are asked, but give in in normally order questions round the the this you.

Example for...

Actually, do let's not this.

In this round, the questions are asked normally, but you **give the words of the answers in alphabetical order.**

1. Which Danish author's fairy tales include *The Little Mermaid* and *The Ugly Duckling*?

2. David Tennant narrated which BBC sitcom about the team planning the London Olympics?

3. Which 2016 film is the third in a series starring Renée Zellweger as a Helen Fielding character?

4. Also referred to as 'PNG', which country is separated from Australia by the Torres Strait?

5.   Which actor and comedian hosted *QI* until 2016?

6.   Which thirteen-part series of dark children's novels was written under the pen name Lemony Snicket?

7.   Who was convicted of heresy in 1633 for believing the Earth revolved around the Sun?

8.   Which 2013 heist flick about a bank-robbing group of magicians stars Jesse Eisenberg and Mark Ruffalo?

9.   In which film does Leonardo DiCaprio star alongside Tom Hanks as the con artist and fake pilot Frank Abagnale Jr?

10. What is the title of this song?*

ANSWERS
See page 244

---

*   Get your best Tina Turner voice ready and really go for it.

GAME 62
HIDDEN IN PLAIN SIGHT

You need: just a willingness to have fun

Players: any number

Scoring: 3 points per answer

Gather around the clues and work together to **find the answer, which is literally hidden in the text.** For example, the phrase 'This scavenging canine will hi**jack al**l the leftover flesh it can find' both describes a jackal and contains the word 'jackal'. But that's where the bold-type help ends.

Take your time.

1. Damon Heta makes this sport a florid art, so graceful is his throwing.

2. This Judaean king ordered the Massacre of the Innocents and other odious nastiness.

3. If you lack energy but have a full day of activities, press on after a tiny cup of this beverage.

4. Many tourists have nice memories of this city on the Adriatic coast.

5.   I like canapés topped with this sauce of basil and nuts.

6.   With audiences reaching 21 million, the Beeb readily commissioned seven series of this family-centred sitcom.

7.   If you are having salad, leave this utensil in the drawer: it's for a different dish altogether.

8.   Having entered the Premiership in 2012, this football club was dreading relegation just a year later.

ANSWERS
See page 244

GAME 63
HOUSE OF GAMERS

You need: nothing extra

Players: any number

Scoring: 2 points per correct answer

Ah, the Mouse Annexe. **We've added a letter to the title of some books and TV shows.** We'll give you a synopsis of the new title, and you tell us what that title is.

For example, if the clue for a book was 'Jean Valjean cheers up the people of Paris', you would reply not *Les Misérables* but *Less Misérables*.

CHILDREN'S BOOKS & STORIES

1. Adopted by wolves, Mowgli starts a new life next to a babbling stream.

2. A young royal sleeps on a pile of mattresses; the fruity foodstuff underneath them all definitely gets squished.

3. A happy little fellow and his friend Big Ears drive around a far-off realm populated by Conservative MPs.

4. In the Hundred Acre Wood, we meet Eeyore, Piglet, Tigger ... and of course their friend, a honey-seeking, poetry-reciting dog.

5. Erich Kästner depicts a gang of Berlin children who catch a thief by finding evidence in his inbox.

TV DATING SHOWS

1. On ITV2, contestants in a sun-kissed villa compete to win a grate-able ingredient of mulled wine.

2. On Channel 4, participants remove their clothing and become increasingly cheesed off.

3. In this American show, a conventionally attractive woman is paired up with a nerd from Athens.

4. On ITV, Paddy McGuinness oversees a surveillance operation while yelling his 'No likey, no lighty' catchphrase.

5. On Channel 5, Paul O'Grady hosts as the author of *The Divine Comedy* looks for love.

ANSWERS
See page 244

GAME 64
DISTINCTLY AVERAGE

You need: pencil and paper; a phone, or someone who's good with numbers

Players: 4, 6, 8, 10 ... basically, an even number that's 4 or more

Scoring: 4 points for every win

You know the drill. Get into pairs. You'll be given a question to which you can only guess the answer. **You and your partner will then take the average of your guesses. The pair that's closest to the actual number gets the points.**

You will then lambast your partner for skewing the average away from your perfectly good guess ... unless of course the lambasting is rightfully yours.

And let's take a moment to remember the difference in guesses as to the value of an Oscars goody bag between Dr Zoe Williams ($750,000) and Ian Moore (a humble $375).*

---

*   The answer is of course $205,000.

1. In miles per hour, how fast could a *Tyrannosaurus rex* run?

2. As a percentage, what proportion of Australia's resident population was born overseas?

3. How many lines does Jason Bourne speak in *Jason Bourne*?

4. According to DVLA data, how many UK drivers are aged over 100?

5. In dollars, what was the drop in the value of social-media service Snapchat 24 hours after Kylie Jenner tweeted 'Sooo does anyone else not open Snapchat anymore?'

ANSWERS

See page 244

ANSWERS

GAME 61: GAMES HOUSE OF ...

1. Andersen Christian Hans
2. *Twelve Twenty*
3. *Baby Bridget Jones's*
4. Guinea New Papua
5. Fry Stephen
6. *A Events of Series Unfortunate*
7. Galilei Galileo
8. *Me Now See You*
9. *Can Catch If Me You*
10. 'Deep High, Mountain River'

GAME 62: HIDDEN IN PLAIN SIGHT

1. Darts
2. Herod
3. Espresso
4. Venice
5. Pesto
6. *Bread*
7. Ladle
8. Reading

GAME 63: HOUSE OF GAMERS

Children's Books & Stories

1. *The Jungle Brook*
2. *The Princess and the Pear*
3. *Noddy Goes to Toryland*
4. *Winnie-the-Pooch*
5. *Email and the Detectives*

TV Dating Shows

1. *Clove Island*
2. *Narked Attraction*
3. *Beauty and the Greek*
4. *Stake Me Out*
5. *Blind Dante*

GAME 64: DISTINCTLY AVERAGE

1. 5
2. 30
3. 45
4. 265
5. 1,300,000,000

SET 16 SCORECARD				
	Player 1	Player 2	Player 3	Player 4
Game 61				
Game 62				
Game 63				
Game 64				
Totals				

WINNER!

SET 17

... in which we dream
of peace in a hut

GAME 65
SPEND A PENNE

You need: a bag of pasta

Players: pairs game

Scoring: You get 2 points each every time your partner gives one of the correct answers, regardless of how much pasta it took to get there.

Wash your hands. Get into pairs and give each player ten pieces of pasta. When it's your turn to play, go to the end of this set and look at the next set of answers, **leaving the remaining groups covered up.**

This is one of those games where you make up the best clues you can think of, hoping to make your partner say the answer.

For each piece of pasta, you may give a single-word clue to any of the answers. Divide them into piles depending on how many words you think each answer will need. You may abandon an answer altogether at this stage. You may not reassign the pasta later. The winner is the pair left with the biggest pile of pasta after each player has had a turn – 1 point per piece.

If you consider yourselves to be advanced players, you may choose to forbid proper nouns.

After you play, *bon appétit*. We tend to prefer a sardine sauce, but it's your supper.

ANSWERS

See page 254

GAME 66
HOUSES OF GAME

You need: nothing else
Players: any number
Scoring: 2 points for each correct answer

The gentlest approach is to take this game in turns, go slowly, and try to amass as many collective points as you can. You *can* do it on the buzzer but when we tried that in the House of Games, things got messy and the reprisals continue to this day. Only this morning, I wrote a 'Where Is Kazakhstan?' set of questions based around the Empire of Aśoka before realising that *someone* had deliberately placed *Muir's Historical Atlas* among the *present-day* books of maps. Whoever it is knows who they are. I said what I said. I'm *not* sorry.

When you answer the questions below, you need to change any plurals to singular, and any singulars to plural. So if the question was 'Which Dickens novel is set in London and Paris?', you would answer not *A Tale of Two Cities*, but *A Tales of Two City*.

1. Which weather-themed hi-NRG floor-filler by the Weather Girls reached number two in 1983?

2. What name is given to the American yeti-like cryptoid also known as Sasquatch?

3. Who was American vice-president from 2017 to 2021?

4. Which Beatles song describes a barber and a fire engine on a Liverpool street?

5. Who created Clarice Bean, and Charlie and Lola?

6. Kevin Costner's directorial debut was which three-hour western of 1990?

7. Which mullet-sporting Steve Coogan character drives a Ford Cortina and dislikes students?

8. What TV genre includes *Doctors*, *Hollyoaks* and *Home and Away*?

9. What best-selling 'Zero Tolerance Approach to Punctuation' features a panda on its book jacket?

10. In *Top Gun*, Radar Intercept Officer L. T. J. G. Nick Bradshaw goes by what avian nickname?

ANSWERS

See page 254

GAME 67
TOTES EMOJI

You need: a phone each

Players: 2 or more

Scoring: see below

Cover up the titles below. **Take it in turns to compose a text message which conveys the answer using only emojis.** Send to everyone else in the room and see who gets the answer first. You get 1 point and so do they.

TWENTIETH-CENTURY NOVELS

1. *North and South*

2. *Anna Karenina*

3. *The Thorn Birds*

4. *Call Me by Your Name*

5. *I Capture the Castle*

AMERICAN SITCOMS

1. *New Girl*

2. *The Good Place*

3. *Two and a Half Men*

4. *Parks and Recreation*

5. *Cheers*

GAME 68

IT'S THAT BLEEPING GAME AGAIN

You need: just this lovely book

Players: any number

Scoring: 3 points per correct title

Three or four generations back, we imagine, we inhabitants of the House of Games would have been put to service working for king and country in one of the huts at Bletchley Park. Or at the very least, begging our commanding officers to have us removed from the European Theatre of Operations so that we could have a peaceful few years in one of the huts at Bletchley Park.

And so we love all the paraphernalia of tradecraft, which is what led us to devise this game, where the clues look as if they've been redacted by intelligence officers.

Study the censored clues, guess what they describe, and then check the answers to see if you were right.

ROALD DAHL NOVELS

1. A naughty little ███ concocts a █████████ potion, which makes his grandmother absolutely ███████.

2. A pair of dirty ████████ play practical jokes on ███ ███████ and live in an utter ████.

3. A rich █████████ is █████████ furious when a local boy and his father poach his ████████ pheasants.

BRITISH SITCOMS

1. A Lord and his servant, a stupid ████████ ████████, find that their ███ing plans always go ████.

2. Newly retired, a grumpy old ████ can't believe he is constantly frustrated by incompetent █████████.

3. Often ██████ed on champagne, ███████ sees that her daughter regards her and her friend as complete ███s.

ANSWERS
See page 254

ANSWERS

GAME 65: SPEND A PENNE
GROUP ONE
Ozone, Tofu, Mount Rushmore, Piglet, Whiskers

GROUP TWO
Dalek, Thong, Charleston, Dutch elm disease, Figure skating

GROUP THREE
Pin the Tail on the Donkey, Emmanuel Macron, Banjo Brie, Fulham

GROUP FOUR
Crochet, *Star Trek*, Gorgon, Gorgonzola, Zola

GROUP FIVE
The Spice Girls, Belfast, Orchids, Pitta bread, The Eurovision Song Contest

GROUP SIX
Asparagus, Henry VIII, A bouncy castle, Emma Raducanu, The year 2000

GAME 66: HOUSES OF GAME
1. 'It's Raining Man'
2. Bigfeet
3. Mikes Penny
4. 'Pence Lanes'
5. Laurens Children

6. *Dance With Wolf*
7. Pauls Calves
8. Soaps opus*
9. *Eat, Shoot and Leaf*
10. Geese

GAME 68: IT'S THAT BLEEPING GAME AGAIN
ROALD DAHL NOVELS
1. A naughty little boy concocts a powerful potion, which makes his grandmother absolutely enormous. *George's Marvellous Medicine*
2. A pair of dirty people play practical jokes on each other and live in an utter mess. *The Twits*
3. A rich landowner is completely furious when a local boy and his father poach his sleepy pheasants. *Danny, the Champion of the World*

BRITISH SITCOMS
1. A Lord and his servant, a stupid turnip devotee, find that their cunning plans always go wrong. *Blackadder*
2. Newly retired, a grumpy old gent can't believe he is constantly frustrated by incompetent tradespeople. *One Foot in the Grave*
3. Often sloshed on champagne, Edina sees that her daughter regards her and her friend as complete fools. *Absolutely Fabulous*

---

* Totally *not* sorry.

SET 17 SCORECARD			
	Player 1	Player 2	Player 3	Player 4
Game 65				
Game 66				
Game 67				
Game 68				
Totals				

WINNER!

SET 18

... in which one of you
lucky people is a spy

GAME 69
ROUND BACKWARDS THE

You need: buzzers or something else that makes a distinctive sound per player

Players: 2 or more, and someone to read the questions

Scoring: 2 points for every correct answer

What a delightful workhorse of a game. A music game may run out of gettable songs that fit the format; a list game can quickly become unwieldy. The Backwards Round, though: ask anything you like and see if you produce a pleasingly absurd answer. It will surely outlive us all.

If you're the one reading these backwards questions, enjoy it. You're *supposed* to sound silly. You also get to be the one who corrects the others if they fail to give the words of the answer in reverse order.

10. Eeyore and Piglet friends his with Wood Acre Hundred the in lives bear fictional which?

9. Trousers yellow wears and Bill Badger with friends is character strip comic which?

8. 1806 in birthday Napoleon's on started landmark Parisian which on construction?

7. *Blood Be Will There* in Plainview Daniel oilman played who?

6. DRC letters the to abbreviated commonly is country African which?

5.   Verne Jules by novel 1869 which in character a is Nemo Captain?

4.   Born Shakespeare William was town English which in?

3.   Kim Lil' and Pink, Mýa, Aguilera Christina by *Rouge Moulin* for reprised was Labelle for hit disco which?

2.   'Man of Brotherhood' including songs with musical which of production Broadway 2011 a in starred Radcliffe Daniel?

1.   Song this of title the is what?*

ANSWERS
See page 269

---

*   Start with the jitterbugs and keep going as long as you need to. Longer, even. (In other words, there's no need to perform a backwards rendition. Unless you can, in which case you should contact *Britain's Got Talent* immediately.)

GAME 70
IS IT ME?

You need: a chair for each player, pencil and paper

Players: 4 plus someone to read the statements

Scoring: 2 points for every correct choice

Each player stands in front of his or her chair. The person reading the questions gives them each a piece of paper with the 'thing' that represents them.

As each statement is read out, players remain standing if they think it applies to them and sit down otherwise.

(For the person reading the statements, we've used bold type for the ones where the player should still be standing.)

SEASONS

Things to write: Spring, Summer, Autumn, Winter

1. I had a UK-wide bank holiday in 2019.

   Spring, **Summer**, Autumn, **Winter**

2. I appear somewhere in the name of an artist who has had a UK number 1.

   Spring, **Summer**, Autumn, Winter

3. An Olympic Games has been held during my three months.

   Spring, **Summer**, **Autumn**, **Winter**

4. I appear in the title of a novel that was shortlisted for a twenty-first-century Booker Prize.

   Spring, **Summer**, **Autumn**, Winter

5 The first two or last two letters in my name are an abbreviation for a US state.

   Spring, Summer, **Autumn**, **Winter**

JOBS

Things to write: Tinker, Tailor, Soldier, Spy

1. I am the title character of a Beatrix Potter story.

   Tinker, **Tailor**, Soldier, Spy

2. I feature in the title of a UK top-ten single.

   Tinker, Tailor, **Soldier**, Spy

3. I am a job which was held by Roald Dahl.

   Tinker, Tailor, Soldier, **Spy**

4. I am an anagram of a Venetian landmark.

   Tinker, **Tailor**, Soldier, Spy

5. I feature in the title of more than one John le Carré novel.

   Tinker, **Tailor**, Soldier, **Spy**

GAME 71
SEE MY GUESTS

> **You need:** to block off parts of the following pages as you go
> **Players:** any number (and someone to check your guesses)
> **Scoring:** see below

You'll see two images of guests from the TV version of *House of Games*. If you can tell who they are straightaway, that's *10 points each*. (Get someone else to check, in case you're wrong.)

If you can't, then there are some questions underneath, of the kind we use in our round It's All In The Name. As that name suggests, this will give you some of the letters of the guest's name. But each time you use one of these questions, *the points available go down by 2*.

Cooperation and inspiration: and you'll all boost your scores.

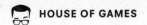

GUEST ONE

For 10 points:

Can you name them?

Answer these questions to get some of the letters in their name.

For 8 points:

Capital of New York state

For 6 points:

Country which seems to think a machete is a good idea on a flag

For 4 points:

The Italian Stallion's surname

For 2 points:

Locale of the rivers where 'we sat down'

GUEST TWO

For 10 points:

Can you name them?

Answer these questions to get some of the letters in their name.

For 8 points:

Word defined by Collins as 'uncontrollable or incoherent talkativeness'

For 6 points:

Opium addict who wrote the lines 'Water, water, every where'

For 4 points:

Tracy who wrote *Girl with a Pearl Earring*

For 2 points:

School title held by Clare Balding and Kate Winslet

ANSWERS

See page 270

GAME 72
INTERNET HISTORY

You need: just the information below

Players: any number

Scoring: 4 points per personage

Cover up the text below, reveal the hashtags one at a time, **and try to be the first to guess which historical figure is the answer.** You'll need to check your own, so incorrect guessers *are* frozen out.

1. #MakingAnImpression
    #BeretSelfie
    #ThrowingLightAndShade
    #GivernyGardenGuy
    #WaterLilies4Lyf

2. #LosingFollowers
    #WhyWyatt
    #TudorTraitor
    #BloodyMary
    #9DaysWonder

3. #SuiteBeats

    #GermanOrganeering

    #BaroqueStar

    #ToccataAndFugueDude

    #BrandenburgerBars

4. #DearDiary

    #QuakingInHerBoots

    #TheAngelReformer

    #FriendofTheQueenVic

    #FiverFace

5. #IKnowWhatISaw

    #Sponsored

    #TravelsWithNiña

    #ShoutoutToSpain

    #NewWorldOrder

ANSWERS

See page 270

ANSWERS

GAME 69: THE BACKWARDS ROUND

10. Pooh-the-Winnie
9. Bear the Rupert
8. Triomphe de Arc
7. Lewis-Day Daniel
6. Congo the of Republic Democratic
5. *Sea the Under Leagues Thousand Twenty*
4. Avon-upon-Stratford
3. 'Marmalade Lady'
2. *Trying Really Without Business in Succeed to How*
1. 'Go-Go You Before Up Me Wake'

GAME 71: SEE MY GUESTS

GUEST ONE

For 8 points: Albany
For 6 points: Angola
For 4 points: Balboa
For 2 points: Babylon
Answer: Gabby Logan

GUEST TWO

For 8 points: Logorrhoea
For 6 points: Coleridge
For 4 points: Chevalier
For 2 points: Head girl
Answer: Craig Revel Horwood

GAME 72 : INTERNET HISTORY

1. Claude Monet
2. Lady Jane Grey
3. Johann Sebastian Bach
4. Elizabeth Fry
5. Christopher Columbus

SET 18 SCORECARD				
	Player 1	Player 2	Player 3	Player 4
Game 69				
Game 70				
Game 71				
Game 72				
Totals				

WINNER!

SET 19

... in which you will see
colours that are not there

GAME 73
MOUSE OF GAMES

You need: nothing
Players: any number, take it in turns
Scoring: 2 points for every correct answer

Back in the Mouse Annexe for the version that's the original and still, some say, the best.

An opposing player will read you a description of a TV show, poem, etc. It is entirely made-up, but **it is also a real TV show, poem, etc. with one letter changed.** So if the description of an artist was 'Marie Antoinette callously remarks that the poor could manage on cod-like fish', you would reply not 'Let them eat cake' but 'Let them eat hake'.

TWENTY-FIRST-CENTURY BEST ACTRESS OSCAR WINNERS

1. It was her performance as a ballerina in *Black Swan* that won the first Oscar for this actress and mail delivery employee.

2. She's been in the Avengers, she won for *Room* and she's a cube of bacon.

3. She's won twice for her performances as a white waterfowl in *Boys Don't Cry* and *Billion Dollar Baby*.

4. When accepting her award for *La La Land*, this actress was memorably enjoying a tiny cake topped with cream and jam.

5. This national treasure's roles have included Queen Elizabeth II, Queen Anne and a swindling fraudster.

RADIO PROGRAMMES

1. During a long day covering cricket, Jonathan Agnew and colleagues discuss co-ordinating their tepees and yurts.

2. Paul Lewis and Louise Cooper advise consumers on the personal financial benefits of collecting the works of a French painter.

3. Members of the public grill a panel of actors – Adams, Schumer and Poehler – about the political issues of the week.

4. A series of talks to advance public understanding, delivered by the guitarist from the Stones and the drummer from the Who.

5. Punt, Dennis and guests take a sideways look at what's happened to female pigs in the past week.

ANSWERS
See page 284

GAME 74
PUT YOUR FINGER ON IT

You need: to block off the answers (end of set) to avoid spoilers

Players: any number

Scoring: 2 points each time you jab well

In the previous *House of Games* book, we achieved something quite magic. We made readers *see colours* on its black-and-white pages. It went like this ...

If is the Indian flag, whose flag is ?

... and again your eyes can now see the orange and green in the second image, and you can tell it's the Irish *trídhathach*.

If you didn't enjoy the concept, I'm delighted to announce that we at the House of Games are doubling down.

For the print version of Put Your Finger On It, gather all players around the book. Get someone to read out the instruction and then count down: 'Three, two, one, JAB.' On 'jab', **all players should point at the part of the image they think is correct.**

1. One person should draw some Olympic rings, then everyone should point to the blue one.

2. Draw a London Underground sign and point to the blue section.

3. Point to the large blue swathe of clothing (we can't expect you to draw this one).

4. Point to the blue ball.

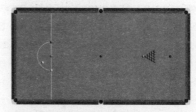

5. Point to the blue section.

ANSWERS
See page 284

Images: Wikimedia Commons

GAME 75
WHO GOES FIRST?

You need: see below

Players: ideally 4

Scoring: 4 points per correct guess

This is one of those 'you don't know, so what's your best guess?' games.

You can't be sure whether it's better to be allowed an early guess (before others get a chance to take the points) or a later one (when wrong options have been eliminated), so there's a randomising mechanism before each question which determines the order you play.

Some of these require a look at a phone. But perhaps you're a group that's playing precisely in order to get everyone *away* from their screens. Perhaps you've finally sat down *for once* to do something *together*. In which case, just do keepy-uppies each time.

Block off the rest of the page, reveal the four options, then guess in the player-order indicated. The answer's on page 284.

1. *Player order: from most to least popular first name in baby births, 2021*

   Which of these films has received the highest rating in a test for historical accuracy?

   > *Selma*
   >
   > *The Imitation Game*
   >
   > *The Wolf of Wall Street*
   >
   > *The King's Speech*

2. *Player order: from highest to lowest Scrabble score for your first name*

   Which of these was available in the UK before any of the others?

   > **Cheese and onion crisps**
   >
   > **Custard powder**
   >
   > **Sliced bread**
   >
   > **Teabags**

3 . *Player order: from lowest to highest number of keepie-uppies achieved*

In the history of the *New York Times*, which article has taken the most 'person-hours' to write?

    Obituary of Fidel Castro

    Edward Snowden intelligence leak

    Interview with J. D. Salinger

    10,000th crossword puzzle

4 . *Player order: from least to most hits on a Google search for your first name*

What is the UK's favourite pizza topping?

    Mushroom

    Pepperoni

    Pineapple

    Ham

5. *Player order: from the least to most time since you last rode a bicycle*

    Who was criticised by the Lord Chief Justice for using the childish term 'Magna Farta'?

    Oliver Cromwell

    Horrible Histories

    Germaine Greer

    King John

ANSWERS
See page 284

GAME 76
INITIAL IMPRESSIONS

If you're the person reading the clues, adopt a medium pace. If you're too fast, the details will get lost. But if you're too slow, the game becomes too easy, as **the first letter of each clue spells out the answer.**

1. Hoffman and Hoskins each plays a baddie

   Once upon a time, these bandits set sail

   Older now, the hero's a lawyer and daddy

   Kidnapping kicks off this swashbuckling tale

2. Perhaps you have been to this 'City of Light'

   Even though doing so calls for quite a long flight

   Rest from the sun in its famous rotunda

   Too many 'bevvies' and maybe you'll 'chunder'

   Heath Ledger was born in this place that's Down Under

3. Cherokee ancestry: this star, she can boast

Her subjects in song, they include Jesse James

Earlier on, her own show did she host

Read that first line again, 'cause it starts with her name

ANSWERS
See page 284

ANSWERS

GAME 73: MOUSE OF GAMES

Twenty-first-century Best Actress
   Oscar Winners

1. Natalie Postman
2. Brie Lardon
3. Hilary Swans
4. Emma Scone
5. Olivia Conman

Radio Programmes

1. *Tent Match Special*
2. *Monet Box*
3. *Amy Questions?*
4. *The Keith Lectures*
5. *The Sow Show*

GAME 74: PUT YOUR FINGER ON IT

1. It's the one in the top left of the arrangement
2. It's the rectangle across the middle
3. It's the main wrap of fabric above her forehead
4. It's right in the centre of the table
5. It's the bottom right-most section

GAME 75: WHO GOES FIRST?

1. *Selma* (100 per cent accurate; *The Imitation Game* got a pitiful 42.3 per cent)
2. Custard powder (1837, way before the others)
3. Obituary of Fidel Castro (rewritten constantly over the 57 years from 1959)
4. Mushroom (two-thirds of the population putting the fungi on top, on top)
5. Oliver Cromwell (apparently he didn't think Magna Carta did enough to redress grievances)

GAME 76: INITIAL IMPRESSIONS

1. *Hook*
2. Perth
3. Cher

SET 19 SCORECARD			
	Player 1	Player 2	Player 3	Player 4
Game 73				
Game 74				
Game 75				
Game 76				
Totals				

WINNER!

SET 20

... in which raised voices are
positively encouraged

GAME 77
JUST SAY ANYTHING

You need: nothing more
Players: pairs plus someone to read the questions
Scoring: 1 point each per correct answer given by both

If you don't know what to say, a guess is always better than nothing. Asked for a Gladiator whose name did not contain an 'E', and never having seen the legendary gameshow, Crystelle Pereira announced she would guess, prompting Stephen Bailey to say, 'If she gets it, I'll die,' and Amanda Lamb to add, 'She will, won't she?'

Offered the chance to sit out the round, Crystelle instead guessed that *Gladiators* might have had an Evangelico. Of course it hadn't, but the general point stands.

If you're reading the questions, alternate them between the pairs. After the question, count down: 'Five, four, three, two, one, SHOUT.' **The pair gets 1 point each only if both of them shout the correct answer immediately. Pausing is not acceptable.**

1. Who was the British monarch during the Second World War?

2. Who did Daniel Craig take over from as James Bond?

3. Which country is the world's biggest exporter of saffron?

4. Which city hosted the Olympic Games in the year of the millennium?

5. What is the penultimate of the seven Harry Potter novels?

6. By population, what is the UK's *third* biggest city?

7. Who has the most Wimbledon ladies' singles titles?

8. Which ingredient of a Waldorf salad provides the protein?

9. In which organ of the body is the loop of Henle?

10. Who was the British monarch during the First World War?

ANSWERS
See page 296

GAME 78
ARTY-FACTS

You need: finger paints (but see below);
phone with a stopwatch

Players: any number

Scoring: see below

In this game, you'll be depicting the answers in artistic form.
The guidance above suggests finger paints, but if all you have is
some large intaglio plates, an acid bath and a vintage printing press,
I'm sure you'll find a way to make it work.

When it's your go, turn to the end of this set and cover up the list
of landmarks, revealing only the next answer. **You then have four
minutes to produce a finger painting of that landmark.** If anyone
can guess what you've been trying to represent, you each get 2 points.

ANSWERS
See page 296

GAME 79

THE ELEPHANT
IN THE ROOM

You need: a noise-making device that
each player can use as a buzzer

Players: 2 or more, plus someone to read out the clues

Scoring: 2 for every correct answer

We remain in the Art Studio, where we do jobs that, hopefully, the TV viewers never even think about, like making Crazy Frog's anatomy suitable for a teatime programme.* Today, we're working on the perfect BOT and CAT images to remind you which sounds to omit as you say your answers.

A reminder: **if the elephant in the room is HAT and you're asked, 'What do you call two cymbals operated by pedal?', you wouldn't say 'hi-hat', you would leave out the HAT and simply say 'hi'.**

Regarding pronunciation (and life in general): be cool.

---

* This is true and it's a remarkably distressing and time-consuming task.

ELEPHANT IN THE ROOM: BOT

1. What country shares borders with South Africa, Namibia, Zimbabwe and Zambia?

2. In monasteries, which monks are in charge of all the other monks?

3. Rob Brydon and Michael Sheen were brought up in which Welsh industrial town?

4. What metaphorical phrase describes lighting a wick twice?

5. When he is stabbed, what curse does Mercutio cast at the Montagues *and* the Capulets?

ELEPHANT IN THE ROOM: CAT

1. Which 'Very Hungry' animal was created by the great Eric Carle?

2. With which band did Cerys Matthews have ten top-ten hits?

3. In what type of improvised jazz singing does the voice imitate instruments?

4. What form of wrestling permits trips, holds below the waist and so on?

5. In education, what does GCSE stand for?

ANSWERS
See page 296

GAME 80
RHYME TIME

You know Rhyme Time. **You get a pair of clues. There's a pair of answers. And the answers rhyme.**

If you're reading the clues, choose someone and read them the first pair: 2 points if they get both right; if not, pass it to the right until someone does, for 1 point.

Either way, play *then* passes to the right.

1. Alfred Hitchcock was prone to making one
    Sitcom where David Mitchell is Shakespeare

2. Actress who played Lauren and Nan
    2019 series starring Helen Mirren as a Russian empress

3. Nationality of Gisele Bündchen and Pelé, among others
    Where cricketers get changed

4. Fruity Viennese relative of baklava

   Controversial hypoallergenic dog breed

5. She was Cleopatra in 1963's *Cleopatra*

   Tinny B♭ noisemaker at the South Africa World Cup

6. Chemical element named after the country where Marie Curie was born

   Chemical element named after what was then a planet

7. Wriggly delicacy, the original cockney 'street food'

   She was Alex in *Flashdance*

8. Nationality of an Ulan Bator native

   He was exiled to Elba

9. Favourite of Elizabeth I who popularised tobacco

   Nickname for Alexandra Palace

10. Voice of Moe Szyslak and Chief Wiggum in *The Simpsons*

    Common warning at self-service checkouts

ANSWERS
See page 296

ANSWERS

GAME 77: JUST SAY ANYTHING

1. George VI
2. Pierce Brosnan
3. Iran
4. Sydney
5. *Harry Potter and the Half-Blood Prince*
6. Glasgow
7. Martina Navratilova
8. Walnuts
9. Kidney
10. George V

GAME 78: ARTY-FACTS

1. The White House
2. Christ the Redeemer statue
3. The Easter Island statues
4. Sydney Opera House
5. The North Pole
6. Balmoral

GAME 79: THE ELEPHANT IN THE ROOM

Bot
1. Swana
2. Abs
3. Port Tal
4. Burning the candle at h ends
5. 'A plague o' h your houses!'

Cat
1. Erpillar
2. Atonia
3. S
4. Ch as ch can
5. General Certifie of Secondary Eduion

GAME 80: RHYME TIME

1. Cameo
   Upstart Crow
2. Catherine Tate
   Catherine the Great
3. Brazilian
   Pavilion
4. Apfelstrudel
   Labradoodle
5. Elizabeth Taylor
   Vuvuzela
6. Polonium
   Plutonium
7. Jellied eels
   Jennifer Beals
8. Mongolian
   Napoleon
9. Walter Raleigh
   Ally Pally
10. Hank Azaria
    Unexpected item in bagging area

SET 20 SCORECARD			
	Player 1	Player 2	Player 3	Player 4
Game 77				
Game 78				
Game 79				
Game 80				
Totals				

WINNER!

SET 21

... in which we ramp
things up a notch

GAME 81
HOUSE OF MEGAS

You need: nothing

Players: any number, take it in turns

Scoring: 2 points for every correct answer

This is our final turn in the Mouse Annexe on this visit to the House of Games.

As we approach the end of your stay, we're going to nudge up the speed on your cerebral treadmill. We're sure you'll keep up.

An opposing player will read you a description of a TV show, poem, etc. **It is entirely made-up, but it is also a real TV show, poem, etc. with one word jumbled up.**

So if the description of a Charles Dickens novel was 'In London, an orphan falls in with a bunch of absolute wallies', you would reply not *Oliver Twist*, but *Oliver Twits*.

Thinking of Charles Dickens novels ...

CHARLES DICKENS NOVELS

1. A long-running court case involves the home of Roald Dahl's illustrator Quentin.

2. Tiny Tim is thrilled to receive a festive gift of a bony seaside souvenir.

3. Little Nell grows up in a peculiar store, jumping around on a single leg.

4. A green-headed duck divides its time between London and Paris.

5. The young Pip comes of age and falls in love with a Swedish environmentalist.

BRITISH SITCOMS

1. Brendan O'Carroll plays a matriarch in a home full of louts and hooligans.

2. In Arkwright and Granville's grocery, there's an informal refusal whatever time of day it is.

3. David Mitchell plays William Shakespeare, seeking investment in his new dot.com enterprise.

4. Peter Kay and Sian Gibson are two rabbit-like creatures on a daily commute.

5. Sheridan Smith and Ralf Little order at the bar for the composer of the *Enigma Variations*.

ANSWERS
See page 311

GAME 82

WE DON'T WANT TO GIVE YOU THAT

You need: nothing extra

Players: ideally 4, plus someone to read the questions

Scoring: 3 points if you name something in the category

You'll be playing in order of how many points you've accumulated so far (or, if you're not counting every point, who's generally looking tasty).

Unlike most of our other games, the player in the lead starts. That's because **the others narrow down the category to the combination where they think that player is least likely to give a correct example.**

If you're the one reading the categories, start with 'Sport' or 'Film' and then follow the options. If you like, you can keep going round until you've exhausted all eight combined categories.

SPORT

Choose WORLD CUP HOST COUNTRIES or SUMMER OLYMPIC HOST CITIES

WORLD CUP HOSTS: Choose 1990s or 2000s

OLYMPIC HOSTS: Choose 1980s or 1990s

FILM

Choose BEST ACTOR OSCAR WINNERS or BEST ACTRESS OSCAR WINNERS

ACTOR: Choose 1990s or 2000s

ACTRESS: Choose 2000s or 2010s

ANSWERS
See page 311

GAME 83
ALL IN THE DETAILS

You need: something to cover the text in this game

Players: pairs game

Scoring: 2 points each whenever a correct location identified

Cover up the list of locations below.

Take turns to reveal a new location from the list of six, then write down the sentences accompanying it, filling the gaps (to the best of your ability).

Then read the 'completed' clues to your partner. They have only one guess. You may not say anything else; at the absolute most, you might grimace at some of the more dubious information you're offering.

Then the next pair gets a go. (The Answers page for this set will give you some gap-filling info that we at the House of Games location think might have been more helpful.*)

---

* If you wish, you can behave like Alex Brooker, who hinted at *The Railway Children* for David Baddiel with the clues 'It is mainly set in the trains. / The main characters' father is into his trains. / It was written by they liked trains.' but we're sure you'd prefer the glory of playing it straight.

LOCATION 1

The answer: The Great Barrier Reef

Clues:

It is located in ...

It can be seen from ...

In 1981 it was selected as a ...

It is built by ...

It is threatened by ...

LOCATION 2

The answer: Giant's Causeway

Clues:

It is next to ...

It was created by ...

It is made from ...

It is ... million years old

It is located in ...

LOCATION 3

The answer: The Prado Museum

Clues:

It is based in …

The building was completed in …

It was originally called the Royal …

It houses important works by …

It is home to artworks such as …

LOCATION 4

The answer: Central African Republic

Clues:

Its capital is …

Its official languages include …

It adopted its current name in …

The countries that it borders include …

Its main exports include …

LOCATION 5

The answer: The Millennium Stadium

Clues:

> It was opened in ...
>
> It is located in ...
>
> The capacity is ...
>
> One of its distinguishing features is a ...
>
> The main sport played there is ...

LOCATION 6

The answer:

Llanfairpwllgwyngyllgogerychwyrndrobwllllantysiliogogogoch

Clues:

> It is located on the island of ...
>
> It is known for photos taken in its ...
>
> A famous couple that has lived nearby is ...
>
> It has a population of around ...
>
> The body of water it sits on is the ...

ANSWERS
See page 312

GAME 84
OPPOSITES ATTRACT

You need: nothing

Players: any number, take it in turns to read the clues

Scoring: 2 points for every correct answer

Let's check in at the House of Games mailroom. The majority of our post concerns three topics:* asking when Dim Sums will make a return (it's in this book!); thanking Richard's beard as a quick way of identifying a repeat broadcast and, most of all: praise for Opposites Attract.

We write back, of course, and share a little secret about this game. In the House of Games's Gallery of Deep Thought, we have a Philosopher-in-Residence, always on call should we need to know what, quite objectively, is the opposite of cheese.

We have our own ideas: Mac, perhaps, or onion, or even wine? Or should we be thinking more broadly? Dessert is a true alternative to cheese. So, famously, is chalk.

No, the Philosopher-in-Residence tells us, after much reflection. The opposite of cheese, we now realise, is … 'No photography, please.'**

---

* Four if you include viewers who see the photographs on the series 1 scoreboard and could swear blind that they remember our having used the trademark avatars from the start. We know. It's spooky. We remember them too. But they never existed.

** Mind you, we sometimes ignore the Philosopher-in-Residence, who, having got hooked on *The Simple Life* thinking it was a documentary about asceticism, insists that the opposite of 'Paris' is 'Nicole'.

One person reads out a category and then some clues. **The clues are *the least helpful ones we could think of.*** So if the category was Pantomime and the clue was 'Pooch in Hats', you would say 'Puss in Boots' for the points.

MAGAZINE TITLES

1. *Solitude*

2. *Beatle*

3. *II*

4. *Modesty Foul*

5. *Unsatisfactory!*

UK PRIME MINISTERS

1. Cleopatra Hades

2. Yoko Minor

3. Oliver Hairyloss

4. Elizabeth Slater

5. Mrs Simpson Arable-Land

TOM HANKS FILMS

1. *Rocky 31*

2. *Viaduct of Moles*

3. *You Have No New Messages*

4. *Cleanse*

5. *The Equatorial Stopping Service*

TYPES OF SANDWICH

1. Villain

2. Spade

3. Copter

4. Thaw

5. Parky

ANSWERS
See page 313

ANSWERS

GAME 81: HOUSE OF MEGAS
Charles Dickens Novels
1. *Blake House*
2. *A Christmas Coral*
3. *The Old Curiosity Hops*
4. *A Teal of Two Cities*
5. *Greta Expectations*

British Sitcoms
1. *Mrs Brown's Yobs*
2. *Nope All Hours*
3. *Startup Crow*
4. *Car Hares*
5. *Two Pints of Elgar and a Packet of Crisps*

GAME 82: WE DON'T WANT TO GIVE YOU THAT
SPORT
WORLD CUP HOSTS:
    1990s – France, Italy, USA
    2000s – Germany, Japan, S. Africa, S. Korea
OLYMPIC HOSTS:
    1980s – Los Angeles, Moscow, Seoul
    1990s – Atlanta, Barcelona

FILM
ACTOR:
    1990s – Roberto Benigni, Nicolas Cage, Gérard Depardieu, Tom Hanks, Anthony Hopkins, Jack Nicholson, Al Pacino, Geoffrey Rush, Kevin Spacey
    2000s – Jeff Bridges, Adrien Brody, Russell Crowe, Daniel Day-Lewis, Jamie Foxx, Philip Seymour Hoffman, Sean Penn, Denzel Washington, Forest Whitaker

ACTRESS:

2000s – Halle Berry, Sandra Bullock, Marion Cotillard,
Nicole Kidman, Helen Mirren, Julia Roberts, Hilary Swank, Charlize Theron,
Kate Winslet, Reese Witherspoon

2010s – Cate Blanchett, Olivia Colman, Brie Larson, Jennifer Lawrence,
Frances McDormand, Julianne Moore, Natalie Portman, Emma Stone,
Meryl Streep, Renée Zellweger

GAME 83: ALL IN THE DETAILS

Location 1: Some Useful Answers

It is located in ... the Coral Sea

It can be seen from ... outer space

In 1981 it was selected as a ... World Heritage site

It is built by ... coral polyps

It is threatened by ... climate change

Location 2: Some Useful Answers

It is next to ... the Atlantic Ocean

It was created by ... lava eruptions

It is made from ... 40,000 basalt columns

It is ... 50–60 million years old

It is located in ... Northern Ireland

Location 3: Some Useful Answers

It is based in ... Madrid

The building was completed in ... 1819

It was originally called the Royal ... Museum of Paintings and Sculptures

It houses important works by ... Diego Velázquez

It is home to artworks such as ... *The Three Graces*

Location 4: Some Useful Answers

Its capital is ... Bangui

Its official languages include ... French

It adopted its current name in … 1960

The countries that it borders include … Chad, Sudan, Cameroon

Its main exports include … diamonds, timber, cotton

Location 5: Some Useful Answers

It was opened in … 1999

It is located in … Cardiff

The capacity is … over 70,000

One of its distinguishing features is a … retractable roof

The main sport played there is … rugby union

Location 6: Some Useful Answers

It is located on the island of … Ynys Môn (or Anglesey)

It is known for photos taken in its … train station

A famous couple that has lived nearby is … the Duke and Duchess of Cambridge

It has a population of around … 3,000

The body of water it sits on is the … Menai Strait

GAME 84: OPPOSITES ATTRACT

Magazine Titles

1. *Company*
2. *Rolling Stone*
3. *Elle*
4. *Vanity Fair*
5. *OK!*

UK Prime Ministers

1. Anthony Eden
2. John Major
3. Stanley Baldwin
4. Margaret Thatcher
5. Edward Heath

Tom Hanks Films
1. *Apollo 13*
2. *Bridge of Spies*
3. *You've Got Mail*
4. *Sully*
5. *The Polar Express*

Types of Sandwich
1. Hero
2. Club
3. Sub
4. Melt
5. Toastie

SET 21 SCORECARD				
	Player 1	Player 2	Player 3	Player 4
Game 81				
Game 82				
Game 83				
Game 84				
Totals				

WINNER!

SET 22

... in which you hope not to sit down

GAME 85

THERE ONCE WAS A QUIZ HOST CALLED RICHARD ...

You need: nothing more

Players: any number

Scoring: 3 points for the first person
to shout each correct answer

Welcome to the Poetry Alcove. Readers and viewers often imagine that our rhyming rounds must be the most fun for the question-writing team. And they'd be right!

For this game, in which **you take it in turns to read the limericks to everyone else**, you're even allowed to deviate from the expected anapaestic metre, and to include as many as three stresses in the third and fourth lines, so long as you've completed in triplicate the requisite paperwork.

This game seems as good a place as any (and better than tucked at the end of the book after the fun has stopped) to mention James Allison, Tom Banks, Abby Brakewell, Katie Burns, Giles Carre, Andrew Credgington, Andrew Davies-Cole, Rose Dawson, the Dawson Brothers, Paddy Duffy, Ian Dunn, Carl Earl-Ocran, James Ellis, Reece Finnegan, Joe Gardner, Elliott Howarth-Johnson, Sam Jones, Ben Justice, Rebecca Kidger, Danny Lorimer, Stephen Lovelock, Rebecca Milloy, Conor Morgan, Dan Pettitt, Mark Porter, Sophie Reid, Jo Sarchet, Sam Shepherd, Jack Sheppard, Sophie Skilling, Kate Sleight, Ria Smith, Oliver Warner, Laura Watson, Tom Wheeler, Apsi Witana, Jack Yeo – in other words, the people who have kindly created all these diversions for you.

1. In this film, they've all gone on vacation
   Two burglars give in to temptation
   But a young whippersnapper
   (And great booby-trapper)
   Arranges their incarceration

2. This sportsman was prone to act odd
   And he captained his national squad
   After devious tricks
   (Mexico '86)
   He claimed he'd been helped out by God

3. This film star's a handsome young lad
   There's a bit at the end that's quite sad
   It's hard to resist
   Somehow spoiling the twist
   And saying why only Cole can see Dad

4. This Trinidad-born woman's a jewel
   She used to do pantos at Yule
   She's been showered with awards
   Now she sits in the Lords
   You could 'Play' when you went to her 'School'

5. This bassist gained much notoriety

   For his public and brash insobriety

   He travelled punk's highway

   Did a version of 'My Way'

   And scandalised decent society

6. This campaigner's not scared of a fight

   In the battle for refugees' rights

   She's a mother to Pax

   In her day job, she acts ...

   ... and directs, and produces and writes!

ANSWERS
See page 330

GAME 86
THERE'S NO 'I' IN OSMAN

When it's your turn to adjudicate, get everyone else on their feet. **Read the category; the other players will take it turns to name things in that category that do not contain the Letter of Doom.**

If they take too long, or mention the Letter of Doom, they must sit down. Last player standing gets the points.

COUNTRIES WHOLLY IN THE SOUTHERN HEMISPHERE

The Letter of Doom: R

Angola	Malawi	Solomon Islands
Bolivia	Mozambique	Tanzania
Botswana	Namibia	Tonga
Chile	New Zealand	Tuvalu
Eswatini	Papua New Guinea	Vanuatu
Fiji	Samoa	Zambia
Lesotho	Seychelles	Zimbabwe

UK NATIONAL PARKS

The Letter of Doom: L

Brecon Beacons	North York Moors
Broads	Peak District
Cairngorms	Pembrokeshire Coast
Dartmoor	Snowdonia
Exmoor	South Downs
New Forest	

WHOLE NUMBERS LOWER THAN 51

The Letter of Doom: I (tick them off as they go!)

One	Fourteen	Forty
Two	Seventeen	Forty-one
Three	Twenty	Forty-two
Four	Twenty-one	Forty-three
Seven	Twenty-two	Forty-four
Ten	Twenty-three	Forty-seven
Eleven	Twenty-four	
Twelve	Twenty-seven	

UK'S TOP 20 TYPES OF PASTA

The Letter of Doom: P

Bucatini	Fusilli	Ravioli
Cannelloni	Gnocchi	Rigatoni
Conchiglie	Lasagne	Tagliatelle
Couscous	Linguine	Tortellini
Farfalle	Macaroni	Vermicelli
Fettuccine	Orzo	

GAME 87
KING OF THE JUMBLE

You need: something to block off parts of the page at a time

Players: any number

Scoring: 2 points for every correct pair

You remember the Naughty Steps? That's where naughty question writers are sent to write music questions for our anagram round. It may not sound a gruesome task, but when you manage to find a song with a title that's an anagram of something else, that's clearable for use in a quiz in all relevant territories, performed by someone who's not on 'The List', that guests have a chance of identifying, and then realise that the anagram is a word like 'tired' that you can't really write a general-knowledge clue for … well, that's when you really do think about what you've done.

Happily, music clues don't work on paper. So **take it in turns to read a pair of clues to the person to your right.**

They must give both answers, and the answers must have the same letters, though not in the same order. If they don't get both, play passes to the right.

Take your time.

1. What Wordsworth's words are

   Surrey town where the Derby's held

2. Seven-sided shape

   When you miss each other's calls

3. Hit with outstretched arms

   Fargo's William H.

4. Fencer's 'Watch out!'

   'Explosive' Bruno Mars ballad of 2010

5. Continental currency, *e.g.* the rupee

   Condiment in a BLT

6. Diego to Salma Hayek's Frida

   Buff-coloured document holder

7. 1994 sci-fi film about an Egyptian portal

   Henley boating events

8. Emergency UK government meeting room with a serpentine name

    Chocolate 'substitute'

9. Watery All Saints number 1 about enjoying the beach

    Equine companion of Superman's cousin Supergirl

10. Childhood home of Jesus

    Book of street maps of Iran's capital

ANSWERS
See page 330

GAME 88
SINGONYMS

You need: just this book

Players: any number, plus someone to read the clues

Scoring: 2 points per correct answer

You remember the Music Room? And you remember the 'paraphrased movie lines' round, Cine-nyms? Put 'em together, turn up the trickiness, and you've got this.

Which songs do the following paraphrased lines come from? Just the song title each time please.

1. It's not solar illumination's fault

    It's not lunar illumination's fault

    It's not fun's fault

    It's dancing's fault

2. I'm phoning you now only

    To express my intense feelings of affection toward you

    I'm phoning you now

    To declare the depth of my feelings

3. (Astronomer) Astronomer

   (Astronomer) Astronomer

   (Astronomer) The Barber of Seville

4. My nickname is based on a temperature scale

   My velocity is 299,792,458 metres per second

5. My rotation is circular

   Can I have some space?

6. Come on in to the Golden State Guest House

   It's a charming spot

   (It's a charming spot)

7. I shall occupy the passenger seat

   In clement weather

   With a sense of self-esteem

8. The reply is airborne, mate

   The reply is airborne

9. Gilded digit!

He's this individual

This individual who resembles a greedy king of Greek legend

10. All your respiration

All your relocation

All your separation

All your perambulation

Will be subject to my observation

ANSWERS
See page 330

ANSWERS

GAME 85: THERE ONCE WAS A QUIZ HOST …

1. *Home Alone*
2. Diego Maradona
3. *The Sixth Sense*
4. Floella Benjamin
5. Sid Vicious
6. Angelina Jolie

GAME 87: KING OF THE JUMBLE

1. Poems / Epsom
2. Heptagon / Phone tag
3. 'Y.M.C.A.' / Macy
4. 'En garde' / Grenade
5. Asian money / Mayonnaise
6. Alfred Molina / Manila folder

7. *Stargate* / Regattas
8. COBRA / Carob
9. 'Pure Shores' / Superhorse
10. Nazareth / *Tehran A-Z*＊

GAME 88: SINGONYMS

1. 'Blame it on the Boogie'
2. 'I Just Called to Say I Love You'
3. 'Bohemian Rhapsody'
4. 'Don't Stop Me Now'
5. 'Spinning Around'
6. 'Hotel California'
7. 'Shotgun'
8. 'Blowin' in the Wind'
9. 'Goldfinger'
10. 'Every Breath You Take'

＊   Or as the locals call it, the *Tehran Hamze-Ye*.

SET 22 SCORECARD			
	Player 1	Player 2	Player 3	Player 4
Game 85				
Game 86				
Game 87				
Game 88				
Totals				

WINNER!

SET 23

... for which conversational Korean
is not necessary, but handy

GAME 89
SIZE MATTERS

You need: pencil and paper for each player

Players: any number

Scoring: see below

In this game, **we give you a category and everyone writes down something they think is in that category.** Cover up the possible answers.

You get 2 points if you've written the longest correct answer of all the guesses (count letters but not spaces, punctuation, etc.).

And you get 4 points if you've managed to find the **longest** of all the possible answers. We've listed them in order of bigness.

SINGLE-WORD COUNTRY NAMES
... beginning with a vowel

Afghanistan	Andorra	Angola
Azerbaijan	Armenia	Israel
Uzbekistan	Austria	Uganda
Argentina	Ecuador	Egypt
Australia	Eritrea	India
Indonesia	Estonia	Italy
Eswatini	Iceland	Iraq
Ethiopia	Ireland	Iran
Albania	Ukraine	Oman
Algeria	Uruguay	

AUTHORS MOST BORROWED FROM UK LIBRARIES

... classified as 'classic' (no longer with us)

Robert Louis Stevenson	Graham Greene
William Shakespeare	Lewis Carroll
Arthur Conan Doyle	Evelyn Waugh
Anthony Trollope	P. G. Wodehouse
Charlotte Brontë	Thomas Hardy
Daphne du Maurier	Enid Blyton
Ernest Hemingway	J. R. R. Tolkien
Agatha Christie	Jane Austen
Charles Dickens	Nevil Shute
Georgette Heyer	Harper Lee
Beatrix Potter	Roald Dahl
John Steinbeck	A. A. Milne
George Orwell	C. S. Lewis

SPORTS AT THE TOKYO OLYMPICS

... as listed on the Tokyo 2020 Results page

Trampoline Gymnastics

Cycling BMX Freestyle

Cycling Mountain Bike

Rhythmic Gymnastics

Artistic Gymnastics

Cycling BMX Racing

Artistic Swimming

Marathon Swimming

Modern Pentathlon

Beach Volleyball

Weightlifting

3x3 Basketball

Skateboarding

Sport Climbing

Cycling Track

Canoe Slalom

Canoe Sprint

Cycling Road

Rugby Sevens

Table Tennis

Basketball

Equestrian

Volleyball

Athletics

Badminton

Taekwondo

Triathlon

Water Polo

Wrestling

Baseball

Football

Handball

Shooting

Softball

Swimming

Archery

Fencing

Sailing

Surfing

Boxing

Diving

Hockey

Karate

Rowing

Tennis

Golf

Judo

CHEMICAL ELEMENTS

... whose names begin with the letter 'C'

Californium	Cadmium	Cerium
Copernicium	Caesium	Cobalt
Chlorine	Calcium	Copper
Chromium	Carbon	Curium

GAME 90
I'M TERRIBLE AT DATING

You need: pencil and paper, a phone with calculator, something to block off the text a piece at a time

Players: 2 or more

Scoring: 2 points for whoever is closest each time

For every event below, write down your guess when it took place. Block off the text as you go.

It's as simple as that.

Except it's not simple, because you're going to be hopelessly wrong on some of them. We'll start with a couple of easy ones.

1. The Gunpowder Plot is foiled

2. The Domesday Book is recorded

3. Henry VIII marries his sixth and final wife, Catherine Parr

4. The phonograph record player is invented

5. Teaching begins at Oxford University

6. Brazil declares independence from Portugal

7. Legendary Italian classical conductor Arturo Toscanini dies

8. The first FA Cup final at the original Wembley Stadium takes place

ANSWERS

See page 346

GAME 91
ONLY FOOLS AND ZEBRAS

> **You need:** nothing more
> **Players:** any number
> **Scoring:** 3 points per correctly mangled answer

It's a game where you give a mangled answer.

First, work out the real answer to the clue. Next, **swap the fruit in the answer for the fruit in the picture. Then say the nonsense that ensues.**

(If you like, you can use a marker pen to force the images into an impractical diamondy shape, like we do on the TV show for reasons no-one can remember.)

1.   What completes this 1990s mobile phone slogan: 'The future's bright ...'?

2. What kind of lorry has a platform raised on a hydraulic crane?

3. Who is the dainty ruler of the Land of Sweets in *The Nutcracker*?

4. In the Pacific, travellers add or subtract a day when crossing what boundary?

5. The Joads feature in which Depression-era 1962 novel by John Steinbeck?

6. Donald Trump was twice called in to what kind of constitutional trial?

7. Which soft drink made its appearance courtside at Wimbledon in 1935?

8. And which two-ingredient dessert is traditionally eaten by spectators at Wimbledon?

ANSWERS

See page 346

GAME 92
BROKEN KARAOKE

You need: nothing

Players: 2 or more (plus 1 to read out the questions)

Scoring: 4 points for every correct answer

Welcome back to our Karaoke Bar. You're in luck: it's UK Hits Largely in Foreign Languages Night. *Skål!*

If you're reading the questions, first give the language. Then read out the initials to the foreign-language lyrics from a well-known passage in a well-known pop song. Try to match them to the song - for example, if the song contains a very long 'yeeeeeeeeeaaaaaaaaaaaaaah', say a curt, simple 'Y', then wait until giving the next letter.

TRY TO STAY ON ONE NOTE. This is not a game about melody. It's pure words, all the way.

If you don't know a song, skip it (or just give it your best shot on the basis that it's not your problem).

And if they don't get it the first time, just read it again, and again …

1. *(Español)* OTYIOTSS
   YVE
   ITTCBP
   YVE
   IYLTCAMISCC
   AMSBTS
   EPF

2. *(Español)* B B
   B B
   B B B
   P B L B
   P B L B

3. *(Français)* V-V C A M C S?
   V-V C A M?
   V-V C A M C S?
   V-V C A M?
   V-V C A M C S?
   V-V C A M?
   V-V C A M C S?
   V-V C A M?

4. *(Deutsch)* A A A
   A A A
   A A A, O O O
   A
   C A R M A

5. *(한국어)* 옵 옵 옵 옵
   에 에 에 에 에 에
   G S

ANSWERS

See page 346

ANSWERS

GAME 90: I'M TERRIBLE AT DATING

1. 1605
2. 1086
3. 1543
4. 1877
5. 1096
6. 1822
7. 1957
8. 1923

GAME 91: ONLY FOOLS AND ZEBRAS

1. '... the future's pineapple'
2. Gooseberry picker
3. The Sugar Kiwi (Fruit) Fairy
4. The International Apple Line
5. *The Pears of Wrath*
6. Implumment
7. Banana barley water
8. Lemons and cream

GAME 92: BROKEN KARAOKE

1. 'Y Viva España'
2. 'La Bamba'
3. 'Lady Marmalade'
4. 'Rock Me Amadeus'
5. 'Gangnam Style'

SET 23 SCORECARD				
	Player 1	Player 2	Player 3	Player 4
Game 89				
Game 90				
Game 91				
Game 92				
Totals				

WINNER!

SET 24

... in which you wish you knew
what your partner's playing at

GAME 93
DIM SUMS

You need: nothing
Players: any number, ideally 4
Scoring: 5 for every correct answer

Two heads are better than one in this game, so ideally you'll be playing in pairs.

And those pairs should take turns to look at the questions below. Each one has an incomplete sum, and four statements. **Each statement describes a number, and your job is to choose which of the statements completes the empty sum.**

PLANETS

_____ + _____ = 9

Oscar nominations for Freddie Mercury biopic *Bohemian Rhapsody*

Grand Slam singles titles won by Venus Williams

Planets in our solar system bigger than Earth

UK top ten singles featuring Bruno Mars

TENNIS

_____ + _____ = 17

Minimum number of games in a complete set

Grand Slam Men's Singles titles for Roger Federer

Olympic medals won by Andy Murray

Total hours played by Isner and Mahut in their record-breaking 2010 Wimbledon match

BROWNS

_____ ÷ _____ = 7

Age of Melanie Brown when the Spice Girls achieved first number one

Gordon Brown's stint as prime minister to nearest whole year

Millie Bobby Brown's character in *Stranger Things*

Novels in Dan Brown's Robert Langdon series

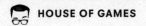

BOOKS

_____ - _____ = 87¼

Dodie Smith's Dalmatians

Joseph Heller's Catch

Adrian Mole's age

Gabriel García Márquez's Years of Solitude

ANSWERS
See page 362

GAME 94
SEE MY GUESTS

You'll see two images of guests from the TV version of *House of Games*. If you can tell who they are straightaway, that's *10 points each*. (Get someone else to check, in case you're wrong.)

If you can't, then there are some questions underneath, of the kind we use in our round It's All In The Name. As that name suggests, this will give you some of the letters of the guest's name. But each time you use one of these questions, *the points available go down by 2.*

Cooperation and inspiration: and you'll all boost your scores.

GUEST ONE

For 10 points:

> Can you name them?

Answer these questions to get some of the letters in their name.

For 8 points:

> Fan of hard rock?

For 6 points:

> It may include ports and reds

For 4 points:

> It's purple and it likes to climb

For 2 points:

Bond likes his ones shaken

GUEST TWO

For 10 points:

Can you name them?

Answer these questions to get some of the letters in their name.

For 8 points:

Mamma Mia! trio: Skarsgård, Firth, _____

For 6 points:

Awful name used when precipitation contains red dust

For 4 points:

Rosalind's love in *As You Like It*

For 2 points:

Orlando's love in *As You Like It*

ANSWERS

See page 362

GAME 95
TWO CLUES IN ONE

This is the round where the *House of Games* question writers are most pleased to be most helpful. **Each clue describes the person in the answer – and has the same initials as the person in the answer.** It probably works best with someone reading out the clues.

We'll give the answers in threes, so try to crack each set, or the whole shebang, before looking.

THEY'VE BEEN KNIGHTED

Micklewhite, Cockney

Cycles Hastily

Imitates Magician

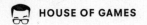
THEY'VE BEEN MADE DAMES

Vibrant Wardrobe

Dances Beautifully

Masterful Baker

FICTIONAL TV DETECTIVES

He's Precise

Seventies Trip

Jovial McEwan

SENIOR SCIENTIFIC ADVISERS

Jaunty Virus-Tropes

Chief Whizz

Praises Vaccinations

BRITISH COMEDY AWARD WINNERS

Lie Master

Caricatures Teenager

Jocular Carpooling

BOND ACTORS

Dominates Casino

Twice Deployed

Decidedly Nonofficial

FRIENDS CHARACTERS

Rich Girl

'Relationship Gap!'

'Could ...' '... *BE* ...'

BILLIONAIRE SPACE EXPLORERS

Recording Business

Journalism Baron

Eccentric Magnate

ANSWERS
See page 362

GAME 96
IT'S NOT ME, IT'S YOU

You need: blindfolds; phone with a stopwatch

Players: pairs game, plus someone to read the events and keep score

Scoring: if you get past the second event, 4; past the third event, 6 etc; 20 points if you make it to the end

In each pair, one of you represents Time Period A and the other one Time Period B - and you're both blindfolded and won't be making any noise.

Someone will read out an event. If you think it happened during your Time Period, silently raise both thumbs; if not, keep them down.

As long as you're *both* right, the person will read out the next event - but **every time you're *not* both right, that person will go back to the first event**, so remember your choices.

Time runs out after three minutes, or when you can't bear any more. Concentrate, and good luck.

TIME PERIOD A: TWENTIETH CENTURY
TIME PERIOD B: TWENTY-FIRST CENTURY

Tony Blair becomes prime minister (Twentieth)

The Queen's Golden Jubilee (Twenty-first)

The Queen's Diamond Jubilee (Twenty-first)

Spice Girls have their last Christmas number 1 (Twentieth)

First Harry Potter book published (Twentieth)

Angela Merkel becomes German chancellor (Twenty-first)

England women's team first reaches the Euros final (Twentieth)

Atlanta hosts the Olympics (Twentieth)

TIME PERIOD A: 1970S
TIME PERIOD B: 1980S

ABBA split up (1980s)

Roger Moore takes over as James Bond (1970s)

Diana and Charles's royal wedding (1980s)

ZX Spectrum computer released (1980s)

Billy Joel sings 'Uptown Girl' (1980s)

BBC launches Ceefax (1970s)

Music CDs appear in shops (1980s)

Spain hosts the World Cup (1980s)

ANSWERS

GAME 93: DIM SUMS

Planets: Mercury Oscar nods (5) + Bigger than Earth (4)

Tennis: Minimum games (6) + Total hours (11)

Browns: Mel B (21) ÷ Gordon Brown (3)

Books: Dalmatians (101) – Mole (13¾)

GAME 94: SEE MY GUESTS

GUEST ONE

For 8 points: Mineralist

For 6 points: Wine list

For 4 points: Wisteria

For 2 points: Martinis

Answer: Martin Lewis

GUEST TWO

For 8 points: Brosnan

For 6 points: Blood rain

For 4 points: Orlando

For 2 points: Rosalind

Answer: Linda Robson

GAME 95: TWO CLUES IN ONE

They've Been Knighted:
Michael Caine; Chris Hoy;
Ian McKellen

They've Been Made Dames:
Vivienne Westwood;
Darcey Bussell; Mary Berry

Fictional TV Detectives:
Hercule Poirot; Sam Tyler;
Jane Marple

Senior Scientific Advisers:
Jonathan Van-Tam; Chris Whitty;
Patrick Vallance

British Comedy Award Winners:
Lee Mack; Catherine Tate;
James Corden

Bond Actors: Daniel Craig;
Timothy Dalton; David Niven

Friends Characters: Rachel Green;
Ross Geller; Chandler Bing

Billionaire Space Explorers:
Richard Branson; Jeff Bezos;
Elon Musk

SET 24 SCORECARD			
	Player 1	Player 2	Player 3	Player 4
Game 93				
Game 94				
Game 95				
Game 96				
Totals				

WINNER!

SET 25

... which has a game that needs
a little more set-up time

GAME 97

RITA ORA'S HOUSE OF GAMES

You need: nothing more

Players: any number

Scoring: 1 point for every correct answer,
1 bonus point if you complete a set

If only we'd called it this on the TV, following our policy of having names that remind players (and indeed ourselves) what any given game's mechanism is. Sadly, we called it The Too Complicated Round and so those about to play it tend to think it will be completely mind-bending, when in fact it is merely largely mind-bending.

Listen to each question. Don't give the actual answer. Give the person* *from the category* that has the same initials as the answer.

For example, in the category Muppets, if you were asked 'Who sang "Dreams" and "Rise"?', you would answer not 'Gabrielle' but 'Gonzo'.

---

*   Or bear.

CLUEDO SUSPECTS

Who played Mrs Thatcher in the film *The Iron Lady*?

Who stars opposite George Clooney in *One Fine Day*?

Which Lancashire-born actor played Friar Laurence in *Romeo + Juliet* and Danny in *Brassed Off*?

Which mischievous satirist was behind *The Day Today* and *Brass Eye*?

DICKENS TITLE CHARACTERS

In 2013, who controversially appeared naked on a wrecking ball in a pop video?

Which star of *The Stepford Wives* and *International Velvet* advertised Fairy Liquid in the 1980s?

Which dashing moustachioed actor starred in *Deliverance*, *Smokey and the Bandit* and *Boogie Nights*?

Which American vice-president accidentally shot an attorney during a quail hunt?

BRITISH OLYMPIANS WITH THREE OR MORE GOLDS

'Walkies!' was the catchphrase of which strict dog trainer of the 1970s and 1980s?

In *Friends*, who played Phoebe's evil twin, Ursula Buffay?

Who co-hosted the Brit Awards with Samantha Fox in the disastrous 1989 ceremony?

Who became well known for sitting uncomfortably next to Piers Morgan on breakfast TV?

CHARACTERS IN GOLDILOCKS AND THE THREE BEARS

Which Latvian-born ballet dancer is known by the nickname 'Misha'?

In Greek mythology, the opening of what released all of the world's evils?

In *Nineteen Eighty-Four*, there is to be no love except the love of whom?

In the book of Samuel, whose height is given as 'six cubits and a span'?

ANSWERS
See page 377

GAME 98
WORKING BACKWARDS

You need: see below

Players: 2 or more, plus a questionmaster

Scoring: see below

Hello questionmaster. The first thing you'll do is **type in something like 'reverse audio online' or 'backwards audio app' to find a way of reversing a recording.**

Next, record yourself reading the questions below (or block them off and record the first few if you'd rather share the fun) – and reverse them.

Then take each player somewhere private and play them the *reversed* audio of some questions a couple of times. Next, record them trying to copy the mangled sounds they can hear.

Finally, reverse *those* recordings. Now you're ready to play. Get someone who doesn't know what the original question was, make them listen and see whether they can work out what they're being asked. If they can, and if their answer's correct: 2 points to them, and to the person whose recording they were hearing.

1. Who played the lead in *The Vicar of Dibley*?

2. What is the square root of 25?

3. Who is the Queen's eldest child?

4. Give an example of onomatopoeia.

5. What kind of creature is Mrs Tiggy-Winkle?

6. Which musical, co-written by Tim Minchin, won the Olivier Award for Best New Musical in 2012?

7. Which are shaped like shells: conchiglie or fusilli?

8. What does an anemometer measure?

9. Is a titmouse a rodent or a bird?

10. What was the most recent leap year?

11. What's the formula for water?

12. By number of episodes, what is the second longest-running British TV comedy series after *Last of the Summer Wine*?

ANSWERS
See page 377

GAME 99
THE ANSWER'S IN THE QUESTION

You need: nothing more

Players: any number

Scoring: 2 points per correct answer

Another game where you may wish to take your sweet time.

The answer is indeed in the question, in bold type: but it's jumbled up each time.

PART ONE

1. If the French exported this wine in a case marked 'Ze stoopeed Inglish call zis "claret"', that really would be **a rude box.**

2. The hero of this classic film does the right thing **since he, at the very** end, returns to his wife.

3. It emits lava and dust clouds: this **molten, ashen unit's** located in Washington State and last erupted in 2008.

4. 1997 saw two UK towns **both handing over** control to this single unitary authority, which became a city in 2001.

5. In the book of Genesis, God creates this river, which is as **pure as the** Garden of Eden.

PART TWO

1. You might say this TV series proves that only **frauds choose** to enter politics: we couldn't possibly comment.

2. On hearing that Hollywood was to adapt his story *To Have and Have Not*, this author might have exclaimed: '**My agent wins here!**'

3. While high notes are out of **my reach**, **aria** performances would be easy for this singer.

4. My all-time favourite BBC Two presenters include the **hard-working classicist** Mary Beard and this colourful chef.

5. You can have a cosy evening here if you change into a **bathrobe, ensconce** yourself in a comfy chair and gaze out at the mountains.

ANSWERS
See page 378

GAME 100
ANSWER SMASH

You need: nothing more

Players: any number

Scoring: 2 points per correct answer

And so we finish, as we so often do, with that old warhorse Answer Smash. At time of writing, we have asked 3,240 Smash questions in the *House of Games*.* Shall we take it to an even 3,250?

You'll be shown an image and asked a question, and you'll combine them to make a Smashed Answer. So if the image showed you Scar from *The Lion King* and the question was 'What poisonous gas has the symbol CO?', you would answer: 'Scarbon monoxide.'

Remember, no points unless you successfully smash the answers together ...

Block off the page, gather round, reveal them one at a time and yell when you've got the answer.

---

* We absolutely do not write these trying to anticipate the baffling answers they sometimes elicit. We genuinely believed, for example, that June Sarpong would give the correct smash (Flangela Merkel) rather than what she did say (Angela Merkel Custard Tart); likewise Gethin Jones (rather than 'Jurgen Klopportunity Knocks', the extraordinary 'Blankety Blank Chequebook and Clock').

1. Amanda Seyfried is the star of which jukebox musical?

2. What is Inspector Morse's first name?

3. Which instrument on the dashboard of a vehicle tells you how far it has travelled?

4. Which UNESCO World Heritage site in Northern Ireland consists of 40,000 interlocking columns of basalt?

5 . What system of government involves a small faction of wealthy people running a country in their own self-interest?

6. Whose autobiography is titled *Before You Leap: A Frog's Eye View of Life's Greatest Lessons*?

7. Which city in Texas appears in the title of a 1971 song by Tony Christie?

8. What three-word term describes a hypothetical global conflict on the scale of 1914–18 and 1939–45?

9. Which round ends with the line 'Life is but a dream'?

10. Which 1990 film had the tagline 'His story will touch you, even though he can't'?

Thanks for playing, and see you next book!

ANSWERS
See page 378

ANSWERS

GAME 97: RITA ORA'S HOUSE OF GAMES

Cluedo Suspects:

Miss Scarlett (Meryl Streep); Mrs Peacock (Michelle Pfeiffer); Professor Plum (Pete Postlethwaite); Colonel Mustard (Chris Morris)

Dickens Title Characters:

Martin Chuzzlewit (Miley Cyrus); Nicholas Nickleby (Nanette Newman); Barnaby Rudge (Burt Reynolds); David Copperfield (Dick Cheney)

British Olympians:

Bradley Wiggins (Barbara Woodhouse); Laura Kenny (Lisa Kudrow); Mo Farah (Mick Fleetwood); Steve Redgrave (Susanna Reid)

Goldilocks:

Mama Bear (Mikhail Baryshnikov); Papa Bear (Pandora's Box); Baby Bear (Big Brother); Goldilocks (Goliath)

GAME 98: WORKING BACKWARDS

1. Dawn French
2. Five
3. Prince Charles
4. [for you to judge]
5. A hedgehog
6. *Matilda*
7. Conchiglie
8. Wind speed
9. A bird
10. 2020
11. H_2O
12. *ChuckleVision*

GAME 99: THE ANSWER'S IN THE QUESTION

Part One

1. Bordeaux
2. *The Seven Year Itch*
3. Mount Saint Helens
4. Brighton and Hove
5. Euphrates

Part Two

1. *House of Cards*
2. Ernest Hemingway
3. Mariah Carey
4. Clarissa Dickson Wright
5. The Brecon Beacons

GAME 100: ANSWER SMASH

1. Barack Obamamma Mia!
2. Pete Townshendeavour
3. Venus de Milometer
4. André the Giant's Causeway
5. Broccoligarchy
6. The Thinkermit the Frog
7. Hamarillo
8. King George the Third World War
9. Mia Farrow, Row, Row Your Boat
10. Eddie 'the Eagle' Edwardscissorhands

SET 25 SCORECARD

	Player 1	Player 2	Player 3	Player 4
Game 97				
Game 98				
Game 99				
Game 100				
Totals				

WINNER!

SET 26

... in which we don't know when
to stop (and then we do)

GAME 101
NOT *THAT* MADONNA

You need: lateral thinking

Players: any number

Scoring: 3 points per correct answer

Actually, we couldn't resist giving you one final set.

This game is based on the tendency, of one inhabitant of the House of Games, to research picture questions as follows:

- Type in the answer

- Take the first image that comes up

- Don't even check if it's e.g. Madonna the pop icon rather than Madonna the religious icon

I won't identify the team member, as we're not a 'name and shame' kind of a workplace.

TYPES OF TROUSER

1.

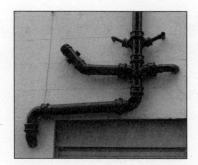

2.

3.

4.

MUSIC ACTS

1.

2.

3.

4.

ANSWERS
See page 393

GAME 102
CORRECTION CENTRE

You need: buzzers, or noise-makers of some sort
Players: any number, plus someone to read out the nonsense
Scoring: 2 for every correct answer

For a gang that prides itself on shunning innaccuracies, we at the House of Games seem to spend a lot of time introducing or welcoming deliberate errors. Exhibit A: this game. Exhibit B: this paragraph. Did you spot it?*

Make someone read these statements aloud. Each of them is completely untrue. **Buzz in when you know how changing *just one word* in the sentence will make it accurate.**

(A hyphenated word is one-hundred-per-cent still a word.)

---

*   It was the extra 'n' in what should have been 'inaccurracies'.**
**   And, to be honest, the extra 'r' in what should have been 'inaccuracies'.

1. Proud Liverpudlian Paul Hollywood has had UK number ones as a solo act, as part of a duo, a trio and of course a quartet.

2. Though we know them as Welsh corgis, the term is not used in America, where they're referred to as 'China hutches'.

3. A beautiful bustier dress embroidered with sequinned fringing in *The Great Escape* helped win costume designer Catherine Martin her third Oscar.

4. Since 2017, French workers have had the legal right to ignore all communication from their bosses during working hours.

5. Les Ferdinand is well known for describing, at enormous length, the grim realities of life in nineteenth-century France.

6. Apart from a brief appearance at the Queen Mother's funeral, the word-famous Neil Diamond has been kept in the Tower of London for decades.

7. Every fourth line in 'Vanity Fair' is a simple list of four herbs.

8. Seven is the only number with the same number of letters as its value.

9. An allegorical investigation of humanity's quest for wisdom and enlightenment, and heavy on Masonic imagery, *The Magic Roundabout* achieved immediate success on its première.

10. Before he played a time-travelling doctor, Peter Capaldi was best known for playing a time-travelling doctor.

ANSWERS
See page 393

GAME 103
WINNING TASTES FANTASTIC

You need: willingness to fight

Players: whatever takes fancy

Scoring: well ... 2, frankly

This is a fast and furious game we play among ourselves where you're given a picture and a three-word question. The questions all begin with the same three letters; why it's this particular three isn't at all clear, you'd have to ask Richard.

If you'd enjoy seeing this one on the telly, let us know.

Cover up the questions that follow and the points go to whoever first yells the answer.

1. Who's this Frenchwoman?

2. What's this fruit?

$$E=mc^2$$

3. Whose thinky formula?

4. When's this fight?

$$12 \times 14 = ?$$

5. What's twelve fourteens?

6. What's this for?

7. Wednesday/Thursday/ Friday?

8. Will this fly?

9. What's 'tempus fugit'?

10. Who's telling fibs?

ANSWERS
See page 393

GAME 104

QUESTION WRITERS' DAY OFF

You need: the information that follows

Players: any number

Scoring: 2 points per correct answer

Ah. You were just promised four bonus games of high-quality – indeed, smashing – questions and answers. The bad news is that Game 104 comes just at the point where we're about to clock off and head off to a pub quiz. The good news is that we have prepared for just this eventuality.

Study the table opposite, **choose a question based on the name and age of the question writer, then turn to page 393.** Our attentive Corporate Affairs department is concerned that child labour laws may make this game in breach of various international treaties, but if we end up in The Hague, we're hoping to rely on the defence 'they're only children'.

If someone gets an answer wrong, other players can shout their guesses. Some of them will almost certainly require multiple guesses.

Cheers!

Alvy, 10	Dulcie, 12	Ada, 10
Nola, 6	Audrey, 9	Bonnie, 3
Sol, 11	Raphael, 10	Joey, 2

Alvy, 10 Is the Amazon the longest river or the one with the most water?	**Dulcie, 12** What was TikTok called before it was called TikTok? a) Mic.Drop b) Musical.ly c) Phone.box	**Ada, 10** Who was the famous mathematician that Ada Lovelace worked with on the Difference Engine leading her to write the world's first computer program?
Nola, 6 What F is this bit of my cat (not fur as she has that all over)? [see over]	**Audrey, 9** Who invented waterproof fabric in 1823?	**Bonnie, 3** Why has daddy got hair?
Sol, 11 Who is a boy in my class and a man who wrote famous songs?	**Raphael, 10** Our government's name for St Kitts and Nevis is 'The Federation of' ... what?	**Joey, 2** What did I make?

Fun fact: this is, we believe, the only question in this book that has also appeared on the TV House of Games.

ANSWERS
See page 393

ANSWERS

GAME 101: NOT *THAT* MADONNA

Types of Trouser

1. Drainpipes
2. Flares
3. Hipsters
4. Bell bottoms

Music Acts

1. Sister Sledge
2. Kate Bush
3. Puff Daddy
4. The Smiths

GAME 102: CORRECTION CENTRE

1. ~~Hollywood~~ » McCartney
2. ~~corgis~~ » dressers
3. ~~Escape~~ » Gatsby
4. ~~during~~ » outside
5. ~~Ferdinand~~ » Misérables
6. ~~Neil~~ » Koh-i-Noor
7. ~~Vanity~~ » Scarborough
8. ~~Seven~~ » Four
9. ~~Roundabout~~ » Flute
10. (the second) ~~time-travelling~~ » spin

GAME 103: WINNING TASTES FANTASTIC

1. Joan of Arc
2. Lychee
3. Albert Einstein's
4. 1066
5. 168
6. Cutting eggs
7. Thursday
8. No
9. Latin for 'time flies'
10. Pinocchio

GAME 104: QUESTION WRITERS' DAY OFF

Alvy, 10: Most water

Dulcie, 12: Musical.ly

Ada, 10: Charles Babbage

Nola, 6: Flank

Audrey, 9: Charles Macintosh

Bonnie, 3: So he can get his hair cut

Sol, 11: Prince

Raphael, 10: St Christopher and Nevis

Joey, 2: A pasta dinosaur

SET 26 SCORECARD			
	Player 1	Player 2	Player 3	Player 4
Game 101				
Game 102				
Game 103				
Game 104				
Totals				

WINNER!

FINAL SCORECARD

	Player 1	Player 2	Player 3	Player 4
Set 1				
Set 2				
Set 3				
Set 4				
Set 5				
Set 6				
Set 7				
Set 8				
Set 9				
Set 10				
Set 11				
Set 12				
Set 13				
Set 14				
Set 15				
Set 16				
Set 17				
Set 18				
Set 19				
Set 20				
Set 21				
Set 22				
Set 23				
Set 24				
Set 25				
Set 26				
TOTAL:				

ONE LAST THING

You're right, we couldn't leave you without one final challenge.
There is a prize* for the first person to tweet Richard the answer:

**If we were playing Hidden In Plain Sight, and the category
was Castles of Kent, the names of which two *House of Games*
contestants could provide clues?**

---

* The prize is honorary citizenship of the *House of Games*.**
** Not redeemable, as it has no value.

ACKNOWLEDGEMENTS

We the question writers would like to thank Stephen Lees, Rachel McLoughlin, Eilidh Keith, Lucy Thomson and Lorraine Kilpatrick and everyone from our team; our director John Smith and everyone at BBC Scotland; our verifiers Richard Morgale, Terri Marzoli and Tim Pollitt*; Susan King, Sarah Boyce, Gemma Whitford and everyone at Remarkable; Yvonne Jacob, Bethany Wright, Phoebe Lindsley, Howard Watson, Paul Simpson, Albert DePetrillo and everyone at BBC Books; Alice Bernardi, Susie Chase, Penny Roberts and the legal team at Endemol Shine UK; Alex McLeod and Eve Winstanley at BBC Daytime and Early-Peak; our ace exec Breid McLoone; someone I'm sure we've forgotten** – and Tamara Gilder, without whom the House of Games would not exist or, worse, would be unmagical.

Finally, we've been talking about how a lot of you came to use House of Games as a salve after the "next slide please" conferences that came, in 2020, to be part of life. Providing even a smidgeon of distraction or comfort meant a lot to us. So, for watching and reading: thanks to you too.

---

*   and if you wouldn't mind verifying this page, that might save potential embarrassment ...

**   Richard. We forgot to thank Richard. Much appreciated, verifiers!

INDEX OF GAMES

All In The Details:	Game 83
And The Answer Isn't:	Game 43
Answer Smash:	Games 4, 100
The Answer's In The Question:	Games 5, 99
Arty-facts:	Game 78
The Backwards Round:	Game 69
Bid Up Yourself:	Game 57
A Blast From The Past Tense:	Game 2.
Broken Karaoke:	Games 7, 39, 92
Build Your Own Question:	Game 6
Can You Feel It?:	Game 16
Cine-nyms:	Game 23
Correction Centre:	Game 102
Crossed Wires:	Game 37
Dim Sums:	Game 93
Distinctly Average:	Games 24, 64
Don't Mention It!:	Game 50
Don't State The Obvious:	Game 54
E, I, E, I ... Oh!:	Game 52
The Elephant In The Room:	Game 79
Five For Three:	Game 32
Fives Alives:	Game 20
Games House Of ...:	Game 61
Gouse Of Hames:	Game 44
Haiku You:	Game 45
Hidden In Plain Sight:	Games 30, 62

Horse Of James: Game 41

Hose Of Games: Game 49

House Of Gamers: Games 38, 63

House Of Megas: Game 81

Houses Of Game: Game 66

I Put A Spell On You: Game 58

Imaginary Charades: Game 3

Initial Impressions: Game 76

Internet History: Game 72

Is/Was: Game 27

Is It Me?: Game 70

It's Not Me, It's You: Game 96

It's That Bleeping Round Again: Game 68

I've Got Those Historical Blues: Game 10

Just Say Anything: Game 77

King Of The Jumble: Game 87

Klaus Of Games: Game 33

Leave This With Me: Game 9

Limericks: Game 85

Look Who's Back!: Game 12

Mouse Of Games: Games 13, 73

The Nice Round: Game 59

Not Rhyme Time: Game 21

Not *That* Madonna: Game 101

Offal Or Waffle: Game 51

Only Fools And Zebras: Game 91

Only One Person Should Read On: Game 36

Opposites Attract: Game 84

The Pen-ultimate Round: Game 31

Pop Art: Games 14, 29

Put Your Finger On It: Game 74

Question Writers' Day Off: Game 104

Rhyme Time: Games 1, 60, 80

The Rich List:	Game 56
Rita Ora's House Of Games:	Game 97
Roonerspisms:	Game 44
Round Backwards The	Game 69
See My Guests:	Games 17, 35, 53, 71, 94
Singonyms:	Game 88
Size Matters:	Games 11, 89
Sounding Off:	Game 48
Spend A Penne:	Game 65
Spoonerisms:	Game 44
Stick It:	Games 40, 55
Tense Squirters:	Game 22
There Once Was A Quiz Host Called Richard ...:	Game 85
There's No 'I' In Osman:	Game 86
Think Like A Question Setter:	Game 28
This Round Is In Code:	Game 15
The Too Complicated Round:	Game 97
Totes Emoji:	Games 47, 67
Two Clues In One:	Game 95
Vowel Movement:	Game 52
Watch Your Breath:	Game 34
We Don't Want To Give You That:	Game 82
Where Is Kazakhstan?:	Game 42
Who Goes First?:	Game 75
Win When They're Singing:	Game 19
Winning Tastes Fantastic:	Game 103
Working Backwards:	Game 98
Wrong You Are:	Game 25
You Complete Me:	Game 18
The Z List:	Games 8, 26, 46